AF443626

CROSS-COUNTRY SKI TRAILS IN THE ROCKIES

CROSS-COUNTRY SKI TRAILS IN THE ROCKIES

John Williams

Contemporary Books, Inc.
Chicago

Library of Congress Cataloging in Publication Data

Williams, John R., 1926-
   Cross-Country Ski Trails in the Rockies

   Bibliography: p
   Includes Index.
   1. Cross-Country Skiing—United States—Rocky
Mountains.   2. Cross-Country skiing—United States—Rocky
Mountains—Directories.   I. Title.
GV854.9C7W55   796.9'3'0973   78-57459
ISBN 0-8092-7573-2
ISBN 0-8092-7572-4 pbk.

Published by Contemporary Books, Inc.
180 North Michigan Avenue, Chicago, Illinois 60601
Manufactured in the United States of America
Library of Congress Catalog Card Number: 78-57459
International Standard Book Number: 0-8092-7573-2 (cloth)
                                    0-8092-7572-4 (paper)

Published simultaneously in Canada by
Beaverbooks
953 Dillingham Road
Pickering, Ontario L1W 1Z7
Canada

Contents

Introduction

God must have made snow on the sixth day just before He rested.

It certainly is the delicious white frosting on our cake of earthly pleasures. Or at least it is for those who find their happiest recreational joys in the great white world of winter.

It is the contention of this book that of all the many ways to enjoy winter, none can equal in return to body and spirit the simple and inexpensive pleasures of a long, gliding walk in the woods on light touring skis.

The physical exercise is nearly perfect. The senses are delighted by the white, cold, gift wrappings on the trees, shrubs, and rolling terrain seen against a bright, blue sky. The spirit is soothed by the crisp silence. Honest appetite and thirst give food and drink their fullest meaning; our companions display a fineness of personality we had only suspected, as we, ourselves, achieve a sort of ageless moment in our lives.

Those are big returns from an essentially simple sport that does not require outstanding physical prowess. It has been said that if you can walk you can ski tour, which is something of an approximate truth. But what is minimally called for is not more than people in general good health can provide: sound heart and lungs, balance, normal coordination, and a bit of extra energy. With that and some snow, as well as the simple clothes and equipment of the sport, you can be off and ski touring.

The ranks of dedicated cross-country skiers have been expanding steadily all through the seventies. Recruits have come from downhill skiers tired of the increasingly large dollar signs and lines of the sport; from backpackers and hikers unwilling to give up their joy of the out-of-doors simply because it has been covered by deep, cold, white powder; from friends and families of committed ski tourers; and from those lucky, curious folks who happened to have observed some cross-country skiers, read an article, or asked a question in a winter sport shop about "those skinny skis."

Until recently the cost of ski touring has been essentially nothing so long as there was sufficient snow cover over land that was not fenced off with serious "No Trespassing" signs. After a snowfall in New York City you can be sure to see a cross-country skier or two working out their city kinks in Central Park. And within easy reach of most snowbelt cities there are federal, state, and private woodlands offering near-endless miles of trails and fields free for the asking.

In recent years, however, a growing number of private ski touring areas have been joining these bountiful options. For a minimum price they provide well-maintained trails, rental and rest facilities, and instruction. In 1976-77 some 400 private ski tour areas charging $2 to $7 a day were operating across the country's snowbelt from Maine to California. Another 80 areas are planned to open during the 1977-78 winter season. These areas are both a response to the growing number of cross-country skiers and a stimulus to the recruitment of new converts. But even at their busiest there have been no reports of serious crowding from any of these areas. The operators are well aware that there is an upper limit to the number of people they can start out on their trail systems without wreck-

Falling can be fun! *Susan Biddle*

ing the very pleasure for which people have come. And because ski touring is by character so quiet and private, just a few quick strides off the trail and away from your group can put you in deep woodland, entirely on your own in a silent, white, winter world.

The beginnings of the history of traveling across deep snow on some sort of "snowshoe" are lost in the ancient blizzards of unrecorded time in northern Europe and Asia. But here and there we catch glimpses of the various winter walking devices that became today's skis and snowshoes. Thousands of years before the birth of Christ, one such device traveled out of central Asia and across the land bridge then linking that frozen land with North America. It was the ancestor of the many varieties of webbed snowshoes used by American Indians and Eskimos.

There is every indication that Scandinavia was the birthplace of the long, sliding wooden runners that became today's skis. Finds have been made of skis dating back to 2000 B.C. Crude sketches have been discovered of humans wielding weapons as hunters and warriors and standing on long boards with curved tips.

With necessity the mother of their invention, skis were conceived of for centuries as just an essential means of winter transportation. The farmer, the hunter, the village and city dweller all needed to get about when the snows lay deep on the land. And certainly the utility of the ski could not have been overlooked by military men over the centuries. The first record of an established ski troop was in Norway some 30 years before the start of the American Revolution.

As skis became more functional and less cumbersome, the chance to enjoy them for sport was accepted throughout northern and alpine Europe. Young people must have started the fun of trying to out-race and out-jump one another while the older or more contemplative found joy in touring across winter landscapes. European immigrants brought their ski sports with them to America. Except for a handful of native American aficionados, they quietly enjoyed their sports, incubating skiing in their communities until the 1930s.

During the middle and late years of the Depression, skiing experienced a small but growing groundswell of interest. It was triggered and helped along by a few zealous missionaries for the sport, many of them immigrants from Alpine Europe. Their efforts helped to establish ski trains in the East and the out-of-the-way Sun Valley railroad destination in the West. Movies and novels also did their bit to put skiing in vogue with the adventurous and romantic.

Though the major focus then and since in the United States has been on downhill skiing, the equipment at that time and the shortage of lifts assured that the skier also would have to walk or climb a good deal. Cable bindings could be adjusted to allow the heel to rise, and the leather boots of the day could be flexed. Skiers also carried skins along with them to be attached to the bottom of their skis to keep them from sliding backward when climbing. These factors, along with a hard core of pure cross-country buffs, continued the traditions of ski touring in New England.

In the gently rolling terrain of northern Midwest states,

home for a large number of Scandinavian immigrants, continuation of the practice and traditions of Nordic skiing were assured. Over the years ski touring gradually snowballed westward to the Rocky Mountain and Pacific Coast ranges. There it joined forces with the pockets of Scandinavian immigrants, mountain men and miners who long had practiced the necessary skills of winter travel along with daredevil downhill races.

By the time Alpine skiing boomed in the United States in the mid-1950s and cross-country skiing came into its own almost 15 years later, there were solid foundations for both forms of

The white, happy loneliness of the long-distance ski tourer. *Bill Scott*

the sport in all parts of the snowbelt. Today, there are some indications that downhill skiing might have peaked. But evidence of the growing boom in cross-country skiing is everywhere.

A major factor affecting both forms of skiing is the increasing cost and crowdedness of downhill ski areas. Another more subtle factor is the changing age composition of the American population, which is not to say that ski touring is only for older folks. Far from it. Young people by the thousands are pinning the skinny skis to their boots to tour, to race, or to mountaineer in the back country. The atmosphere, however, of the contemplative though athletic serenity through which ski tourers glide just might have more appeal for the more mature lover of the great outdoors.

This book will examine ski touring opportunities in the High Country of Colorado, Utah, New Mexico, and Arizona. And while much of what cross-country skiers will find in these regions is the same as in other snowbelt areas of the United States, some subtle and not so subtle differences will be noted and explored.

The principal features of this cluster of four states in the Rocky Mountain West as they affect ski touring are the huge expanse of the area and the length of winter season. These two factors separately and together produce a number of conditions that are not all found in other parts of the snowbelt. A lifetime of cross-country skiing probably would not be sufficient to explore other than in a meager way all of the possible trails that wind across the fields and pastures, foothills and ridgelines, and deep forests, aspen groves, meadows, and snowfields of the High Country.

Taking advantage of a trail break on the way down to the town of Red Cliff, Colorado. *Susan Biddle*

For about half the year this is a world covered by heavy snows. (Even dry winters such as 1976-77 produce more than enough snow for cross-country skiers to get out and stretch.) The length of the good snow season is further extended by the great range in altitudes. When the 7,000-foot level at the bottom of the mountain has turned into a sea of mud under April's hot sun, with lifts ground to a halt, ski tourers in light shirts are gliding along at the 11,000-foot line on vast expanses of eminently skiable snow.

This expanse, this ability to really get away from it all into wilderness, offers a wide range of pleasures to the practiced and sensible ski tourer as well as a self-destruct kit to the unwary and unlearned. It's easy to have fun. But it is just about as easy to get into trouble. And the fact is that in almost all cases the latter happens needlessly. A lack of good sense enhanced by a lack of preparation is about all that is needed to run up the odds for becoming part of some unpleasant statistics.

An important snowy-weather item for the Rocky Mountain ski tourer to keep an eye on is the change of weather. In the High Country it can change with a suddenness that would surprise a sailor. The wind rises sharply, dark clouds storm over the western ridgeline, and a sudden blizzard shrinks the cold white world down to the ghost forms of the few nearest trees. If you and your companions are sensibly prepared and the tour leader is knowledgeable, it is just another marvelous Rocky Mountain ski touring adventure. But if not, well, then it can be concern and trouble, and, possibly, pain or worse.

Snowmobiles have reduced the ranks of those using cross-country skis in their work: foresters, game and wildlife managers, communications maintenance people, Park Service rangers, and personnel of the government agencies involved in watershed management. There are, though, probably more people using cross-country skis as necessary transportation in the High Country than in any other region of the nation's snowbelt. And included in this group are the new and growing breed of mountain men and women who seek seclusion in cabins, houses, and small farmsteads well away from infrequently plowed, narrow country roads.

Almost all of the Alpine ski areas in the four-state region now offer ski touring instruction and guides either as part of their own programs or through independent operators. Information folders on these schools and guide services may be obtained by contacting the resort's information service. These services usually handle lodging reservations as well for the downhill hordes and the small but growing brotherly band of ski tourers.

Convenient cross-country trails generally may be found cutting through or starting at the edge of the base area or town. For example, each of Colorado's big three resorts, Aspen, Vail, and Steamboat, has a system of trails linked to the base area or town that offers a smorgasbord of practice runs and part-day outings. And, nearby, a number of touring trails start treks of varying degrees of difficulty through Forest Service land.

The ski-touring class gets assembled. *Sven Wiik*

These resorts are just the obvious ski touring areas available to you in the Rocky Mountain West. The national and state forests and parks throughout the region that catch sufficient snow all have trail and road systems open to ski tourers and often snowmobilers as well, which is not always a crying shame if they leave you a lightly packed trail in deep, powder snow. Some trails, however, are restricted to cross-country skiers, and it is nice to know which ones they are. We will look at that later.

Serious ski mountaineers almost certainly will venture across one or more of the back country or wilderness stretches of the national forests of the region. And then in the lower elevations there are private lands that lend themselves to beautiful cross-country day tours. But be sure to ask permission to enter or know beyond a doubt that the owners permit ski tourers. The principle of permission also holds for the smaller plots of private land that might lie in the way of your most direct travel. If in doubt, circle about. That's just part of the Golden Rule for cross-country skiers.

Terrain for all levels of competence exists in abundance. Be you a raw beginner, a slightly practiced novice, an intermediate with a couple of seasons under your skis, or a fully experienced expert and ski mountaineer, there is an inexhaustible supply of relaxing or challenging ski country. The dictates of good sense recommend that beginning and novice skiers either join a guided class or check out trails they plan to tour in guidebooks such as this. And do not forget to check with qualified locals before starting out. In fact, it is wise for even experienced cross-country skiers to check with local people in areas they are unfamiliar with or have not visited for a period of time. Conditions do change.

One changeable condition of High Country skiing is the seasons within the winter season. One winter will never be a perfect repeat pattern of the one gone before. Over the years, however, certain average seasonal variations have been recorded, such as January thaw. Knowing about them can be of help in planning your winter touring season. And knowing that you cannot count on the weather will keep you from any disappointing surprises. More on that later in the book.

A final introductory note about the winter High Country of Colorado, Utah, New Mexico, and Arizona: it is a very big country and can be very wild and cold in winter. So make your travel plans accordingly. Plan ahead, plan carefully, and plan conservatively, particularly if your travel involves a great amount of winter driving.

With luck we have waxed your mental skis in this introduction so that you will be able to glide without a speck of trouble right on through the chapters of this book and into the great outdoors. What we will not discuss in this book is cross-country skiing technique. There are many fine books and fine instructors to take care of those matters. The only "how to" we will deal with is how to be a comfortable, safe, knowledgeable ski tourer. Better to avoid the snowy woods and fields if you stand a chance of being cold, hungry, thirsty, or in danger for lack of understanding or proper preparation.

What you will find here are brief guides to and descriptions of the widest possible range of ski trails in the four-state region. This material has been collected from the U.S. Forest Service, the U.S. Park Service, ski area operators, ski tour schools and guides, the U.S. Ski Association, and any number of dedicated ski tourers who have shared in writing their impressions of particular trails. The book also includes the personal experiences of the author and his ski-touring friends and acquaintances. To all of these sources, my sincere thanks.

Part 1

The Principles

1— The Outer Man, Woman, and Child

For those of you who are well-practiced and equipped cross-country skiers (but who are contemplating skiing the Rocky Mountain High Country for the first time), this chapter is offered in the belief that there is always something new to learn. At the least, it will confirm that the fashion principle of cross-country skiing remains "warm is wonderful; comfortable is beautiful."

For the beginner, the information in this and the following chapter is essential to a long and happy life on ski-touring trails.

Getting into tour skiing requires some equipment, some proper clothing, and some accessories. But you shouldn't need a bank loan just to get ready. If you are a reasonably active outdoor person, you probably already own most of the clothing you will ever need. As for equipment, a low of $80 and a high of $160 will get you good to excellent skis, poles, boots, and bindings. It probably would be wise, however, to rent equipment your first few times out. First off, you will have the chance to confirm that you are going to love your new sport.

Not much likelihood that you won't, but why risk $100 more or less. And second, you will have a chance to explore the principal question about cross-country skis: to wax or not to wax. Technological man is moving in on tradition. It is not a flip of of the coin question, however. After some experience with both, you will be able to make a choice that will keep subsequent nagging doubts out of your tracks.

Skis, Poles, Bindings, and Boots

Some years back, it wasn't much of a problem when you decided to go out and buy cross-country skis. Most were made by Scandinavian manufacturers who had long and comfortable reputations. Wood was the material, and the ski had to be waxed to make it stick and slide. Your intended use—mountaineering, touring, racing—established the model to buy. And

Friends share a relaxed moment at the Devil's Thumb Ranch and Cross-Country Ski Center in Fraser, Colorado. *Sidney Fingerman/Devil's Thumb Cross-Country Ski Center*

so it went in a "not-much-choice" way with other basic equipment: poles, bindings, and boots.

But today there are dozens of manufacturers offering hundreds of different ski models. Do not despair. Though equipment has gone supermarket, the underlying questions and answers have not changed. It is still a matter of what sort of cross-country skiing you plan to do and how much you wish to spend. When you know those answers, you will find that the sales people in most of the stores dealing in skis and mountaineering equipment are well prepared to help you select the equipment that fits your needs.

At most outfitters you will find light, medium, and heavy cross-country touring skis. A few more will also carry the super-light racing skis and the heavy-duty mountaineering skis with metal edges. The construction materials range from solid wood and wood laminates to fiberglass/wood laminates and solid fiberglass. What is offered, essentially, is a strength-to-weight ratio against cost. Generally, the lighter and stronger a touring ski, the more desirable it is. But it also costs more. All touring skis, however, are light compared to downhill skis. Just heft the two types in a shop and see.

When you get around to buying your own skis after renting, you will find the bottom of the line at about $30 for solid wood skis. Wood laminates and wood and fiberglass combinations run in the $40 to $60 range. All-fiberglass skis cost between $65 and $85. It is not that you can't spend more if you wish. Prices climb well above these figures, but there is no need for most cross-country skiers to follow them.

The second question after deciding on materials and price range is whether or not to delve into the not-so-deep mysteries of waxing. The proper wax on the ski bottom "grabs" the surface of the snow and lets you push forward across the flat or uphill. It also lets you glide forward. Essentially, you need a hard wax for cold, dry snow and a soft wax for soft, wet snow. There also are waxes for the gradations in between. You will find either a certain pleasant science and sorcery about this aspect of cross-country skiing or it will be a confounding irritation. Quite quickly, your personality will let you know what it has to say about the matter.

If your response is the first reaction, you will find plenty of literature to explore and wax brands and types to sample. As you go about this artistic science, an open and inquiring attitude will bring you the wisdom and advice of fellow waxers. If your reaction falls into the second category ask the store clerk about the relative merits of mohair strips, fish-scale bottoms, and stepped kicker areas. The only generally acknowledged disadvantage of the bottoms that do not use wax to grip for the forward stride is that they are somewhat slower on descent. That might not be all bad.

One nice, and often unmentioned, benefit gained from waxing skis is that now and then you are required to take a trail break and re-wax. The break not only is restful but it gives you a quiet chance to "feel" your surroundings and to contemplate again the whole day's plan.

On the way to Red Cliff, Colorado, a break to re-wax skis can provide an opportunity for comtemplation. *Susan Biddle*

The old standard for measuring skis—from floor to heel of raised hand—is still the best for cross-country skis. Quite possibly as a novice you would get along better on a somewhat shorter pair. Starting out with short skis has worked very well in downhill ski instruction. Turning at fair speed is the be-all and end-all of Alpine skiing. The short ski lets the beginner experience this maneuver early on and in reasonable safety. But in Nordic skiing a difference in length is not all that important. The beginner learns the cross-country basics of balance, kick, and glide so rapidly that in very little time the proper length ski is the proper ski to have.

Cross-country ski poles add push and balance to your snow travels. It is well to try a few rental poles—bamboo, metal, or fiberglass—before plunking down your money. In addition to being the proper length—floor to outstretched underarm— they should be light, strong, and flexible. Don't try to carry over a pair of downhill poles to the sport; they are just too heavy for all day workouts, and if they are your own downhill poles, they will not be the right length.

Cost again will be a factor as to which poles you buy. Ideally, however, you will let the weight-to-strength ratio be your guide. Cross-country provides a perfectly fine workout without the need to carry along any excess weight, be it in equipment, backpack, or your own body. Also check that your poles have adjustable straps. As you go from heavy mittens to bare hands as the weather allows, you will want to be able to adjust the straps for a proper grip.

Boots and bindings for touring skis now are almost universally standardized to the extended, squarish sole at the toe that locks into a three-pin binding. Holes in the bottom of the sole align with the pins, and the simple binding clamps boots and skis together. Release from these bindings may be accomplished by using the tip of the ski pole.

Boots today are made from synthetic materials as well as from leather, and they are cut to fit below and above the ankle as well. Here, again, you have a decision to make based on personal inclinations or the advice of other ski tourers and ski shop people. But no matter what style you buy, make sure the boots fit snugly over the doubled-up pair of socks you should wear when touring. It also is smart to break in new boots before touring by wearing them around the house. What you are after is a flexible, comfortable, snug fit. What you do not want are sore spots developing midway through a long ski tour.

This standard boot and binding combination for general touring, with the boot held to the ski at the toe, depends only upon the strength of the boot sole to keep your foot in line with the ski. While this works very well under most conditions, when manuvering downhill it can happen that the boot will twist to such an extent that it will either pop out of the binding or you will pop out of the boot. Usually you are heading for a fall about this time, an event of little threat in everyday ski touring. However, if you are packing heavy loads into back country or are ski mountaineering, it is better to have another type of ski/binding combination, one that will give you more ski surface and increased lateral control through a heel cable. With most of these types of bindings you can lock your heels down for steep descents.

Clothing

Once your equipment decisions are resolved, it is time to examine your wardrobe. Warm, dry, and comfortable while active are the merits to be sought from ski-touring togs. Of course, there is nothing wrong with looking nice. It isn't that cross-country skiing is anti-fashion, it's just that there is no good reason to look as though you are suiting up for a space shot. Downhill skiers need the protection of those classy, padded, body-covering outfits since so much of their time is spent waiting in long, cold lines or riding long, cold lifts. Cross-country skiers generate their own heat needs and then some as they go snow gliding. It is important to be able to adjust your clothing so that you retain enough heat to beat the cold but not so much that you break out into a sweat. How to do that? Use the ''layers'' principle. Dress so that you can remove or add clothing layers as your own body temperature or the air temperature changes.

Cotton next to the skin just cannot be beaten for comfort. And it is the most effective fabric for absorbing the moisture your body produces even when at rest. A cotton T-shirt and shorts for men and bra and pants for women are strongly recommended. Another option is the open-knit cotton underwear developed in Scandinavia. Its principal function is to provide a still air layer between the skin and the next over-garment.

Since your homework already will have told you the likely temperature range and winds to expect on your day tour, the next item of clothing will or will not be long underwear, tops and bottoms. You will find these available in cotton and cotton/synthetic mixtures. Not very often will you need double layer or padded long underwear. Some people prefer a fine wool top garment, crew or turtleneck. But whatever your choice, on a cold winter's day the full body cover of long underwear is the vital second layer of your warm, dry, comfortable costume.

A light cotton or wool workshirt comprises another layer, and on a sunny, windless day it might well become your outer garment as you build up body heat. A shirt has its own built-in temperature controls since you can roll up the sleeves and unbutton the front should your exertions make that necessary.

A medium-weight wool sweater will serve as a fine top layer on an average, sunny winter's day. In the West a down vest often will be worn instead of or over a lightweight sweater. That is a matter of preference and personal response to the cold. Other top garments you will need include a windproof, water-repellent shell (not waterproof; it must "breathe") to meet those conditions, and either a heavy wool sweater or a ski jacket to throw on when you stop to rest or arrive back at the trail head after your tour.

Corduroy jeans are probably the Western ski tourer's pants of choice. But the traditional corduroy or wool knicker and high wool sock are much in evidence also. Both allow ease of movement and sufficient warmth when worn over long under-wear. And don't forget a pair of gaiters made of some waterproof fabric and designed to keep snow out of your boots. Wet feet quickly become cold feet, and there goes the fun. Most ski tourers who wear knickers use the low, ankle-height gaiter. Cross-country skiers in jeans or other long pants generally wear a gaiter that ends just below the knee. Pants bottoms are tucked into them. If you simply are going to run on a packed track, you won't, of course, need gaiters at all.

As we said earlier, you probably already have just about all the clothing, including wool hat and mittens or gloves, that you will need for everyday ski touring. However, if you plan to set out on overnight or longer ski-touring trips, you might want to look into some of the special clothing that a good back-country or mountain-outfitting store can offer. For example, as protection against biting winds or blizzard conditions, a wool balaclava to pull down over your entire head and onto your shoulders is certainly worth carrying along in your pack.

And a little emphasis here on the marvels of wool can only do good. Even when wet, wool retains a large part of its capability to hold in your body heat. Cotton corduroy jeans are fine for a sunny day hike, but if you know you may get cold and wet during the day, or if you are going off overnight or longer, be sure you wear woolen knickers or trousers or have a pair with you.

Even on a day or half-day trip you probably will want to sling on a light pack for carrying waxes, energy snacks, oranges for thirst, an emergency repair kit that includes a replacement ski tip, camera, and sun-tanning or sun-blocking lotions or creams. If there is room, you can stash your heavy sweater or jacket in your pack. If not, tie it to the outside or to your belt. That's better than tying it around your waist where it will add a partial, unwanted layer. Be sure that your pack straps are padded or wide and substantial enough to ensure that you do not wind up with skinny "tourniquets" binding your shoulders. Nothing is more uncomfortable, except perhaps a fold in your sock.

As for socks, day conditions and personal preference will decide what you will wear. But one good combination is a light, white cotton athletic sock with a heavy wool sock over it. This will provide your feet with protection from the cold and from friction with your boots, and both layers of socks wick moisture away quite well. It is not a bad idea to carry extra socks in your pack since it is always possible, particularly in the spring, to run into a lightly covered creek or sump hole as you stride across a meadow or dip through a draw.

The other body extremities to pay attention to are the hands and head. No matter how warmly bundled you might be on a very cold day, an uncovered head can cost you a dangerous amount of body heat. In turn, a covered head will let you dress more lightly, perhaps even saving a layer or allowing you to open your jacket as you ski along. Your head, in effect, can serve as a thermostat to maintain the proper body heat at your core. If the air temperature drops and you feel the start of a chill, pull your wool hat on. Alternatively, if you are puffing a bit with the climb and your body temperature is on the rise, off with your hat.

Hands can play a similar role, but not with the same efficiency since they are well away from the trunk and the big thigh muscles, which generate much of our body heat. Generally, you will want your hands covered, with mittens on really cold days and with light gloves on balmy ones. But if you find yourself overheating, take your gloves off along with your hat and see if that won't do the trick. If the heat continues to

A group leaves for a ski tour at the Devil's Thumb Cross-Country Ski Center, Fraser, Colorado. The Center is also the training site for the U.S. Cross-Country Ski Team. *Sheldon Fingerman/Devil's Thumb Cross-Country Ski Center*

build up, however, you will have to start shedding clothing layer by layer.

Should you be one of those people who enjoy a little more color and style in your costume than these suggested everyday clothes will provide, rest assured that the ski shops are prepared to part you from your money with lines of designer ski-touring clothes, which is not to say that there is anything wrong with a bit of style and brightness in your outfit. A distinctive splash of color might well be a safety factor under certain touring conditions. Just as equipment manufacturers have rapidly extended the lines of touring skis, the sports clothing people have recognized the cross-country boom. Almost all of what you will find is sensibly if fashionably designed as well as utilitarian. But it will not really improve on the warm, dry, comfortable standard of everyday outdoor clothing. The decision is basically one of the pocketbook, though probably most ski tourers would find it a shame if their sport lost its knockabout look and took on the shiny newness of space-age downhill costumes.

You probably already own a pair of sunglasses that will function quite well for ski touring. But be certain that the lenses are large enough to give your eyes plenty of protection. If they are not the mirrored kind, color is important. The tint should be gray, gray-green, or green. You want to block as much ultraviolet as possible and reduce the total amount of light. But it is also nice to see the winter countryside in its natural colors, and these tints work well that way. If there is a heavy overcast, amber or yellow lenses will improve your view of the snow surface and enable you to see bumps and rolls. Polarized glasses, fine for water and highway glare, are of little use with snow since they are designed to block glare from only one direction. When it is snowing and the wind is up, you probably will need goggles. Make sure they have ventilators; otherwise they will fog up in no time.

Another accessory you might wish to consider as an alternative to or in addition to your backpack is a fanny-pack, which straps around your middle and rides on top of your buttocks. For a short trip or even a day trip when the weather is forecast to be good, you easily might be able to carry all of your extras—waxes, ski tip, food—in it. And though oranges and even snow may be used to quench your thirst, it is not a bad idea to carry along a plastic water bottle or a wineskin with water or one of the powder-mix drinks. If you buy the type of plastic bottle that has its cap attached to the neck by a stout plastic strap, you will be able to dangle the bottle from your belt by passing the cap around it and back onto the bottle. Also, if your water supply runs low and you ski near a creek with open water, you can safely replenish without chancing a wet foot by weaving the cap through the basket of your ski pole and then reaching out to the water. A bit of string will fasten a wineskin to your belt, preventing it from swinging as you ski.

As your experience on touring skis increases you will establish for yourself those little procedures and conveniences that go toward assuring good days in the snow. Some you will discover for yourself and others will be learned by observing your companions. It is quite possible that you will invent some little trick or technique that you can share with your fellows. Getting along in comfort is a very important part of ski touring.

2— The Inner Man, Woman, and Child

Physical and Mental Conditioning

Being in good shape means being able to sustain demanding physical activity over an extended period of time. The heart, lungs, and muscles all must be able to do their share. Young children constantly on the run and athletes and laborers putting out daily strenuous effort need have little concern about being in shape. But the rest of us need something more than the daily effort to bend over and tie our shoes.

Acceptance of this definition of good shape has spread rapidly during the past decade. Bike sales have skyrocketed, joggers are everywhere, swim clubs are doing a land-office business, and even walkers are matching this new pace. It only can be hoped that these hordes concerned with their well-being have established a daily schedule for their pursuit of good health. Daily moderate exercise for a reasonable period of time is the ticket. You are seeking a comfortable tired glow from your efforts, not exhaustion. Sporadic, explosive exercise is liable to put you in the hands of a doctor.

It is not really too hard to get into good shape—assuming there is nothing basically wrong with you. If you harbor any doubts or are over 40 and something of a stranger to regular exercise, visit your doctor before commencing a daily regimen. But if you are basically sound, it won't take long for a daily stint of stretching your muscles and stressing your heart and lungs to put you in shape for cross-country skiing and a longer and healthier life. When the season lets you add regular touring to your fitness schedule, you will have energy to burn.

But we all are different. It is sensible not to put too competitive an edge into your daily jogging, swimming, or cross-country running. The pace you want to set is the one that best suits your needs. Just because you can run cross-country for four to six miles does not mean you should try to run a four to six minute mile.

If you have a track or field for ski-touring practice, set a pace that puts you under stress but not strain. When out ski

Smiles give evidence of the delight of competition at the Devil's Thumb Cross-Country Ski Center, Fraser, Colorado. *Sheldon Fingerman/Devil's Thumb Cross-Country Ski Center*

touring with a group, the pace should be that of the slowest skier, even if that is you. Don't let pride push you beyond your comfortable level for sustained effort. It just is not safe for you and your cross-country friends; they might have to carry you out. However, there is nothing to say that you cannot increase your stamina level. Regular, daily workouts are the only way to do it. In no time at all it will be you cutting your speed to keep the group together.

Without getting into a thicket of details, it must be noted that a proper diet is an important part of getting into and maintaining good shape. The body needs good fuel to burn in order to build a strong, energy-efficient system of heart, lungs, blood vessels, and muscles. One nice thing about the work required to attain and maintain good shape is the appetite it earns. If you treat this healthy appetite with good sense and moderation, you can add to, subtract from, or maintain that other shape that is more related to your belt size than your stamina.

To attain and maintain a healthy body, it is a great help to have a healthy mind. Just what that means for you most likely will be different from what it means for me. But it does not mean that you can't be a little bit crazy or have some pretty weird views on things. Some very controversial figures of American life go in for cross-country skiing. But what they share with you and their fellow ski tourers is joy in the sport and in nature. And that is a healthy mental outlook by any definition.

Though cross-country skiing can demand very hard work from you, it should never be a drudgery. With a happy, healthy mental outlook you can challengingly imagine that you are headed for the top of Mt. Everest as you make a tough herringbone or sidestep up a steep grade. And chatting about your observations or happy fantasies as you stomp or glide along with your fellow skiers is one of the very special pleasures of ski touring. Talking as you travel, the immediate sharing of your responses to the world around you, is just one more of ski touring's special pleasures that is lacking in downhill skiing.

Venturing into the Rocky Mountains in the winter is a special adventure.

A little quiet singing and daydreaming doesn't hurt your spirits either. I remember one silent, snowing day deep along the Continental Divide when a friend, close but infrequently seen, and I slid away from the trail and into a spruce cluster for a short break and a chance to nibble and sip. We were settled quietly, resting and dreaming, when a ripple of wind through the snow seemed to set dark gray things moving on an opposite slope that was covered with wintering aspens and evergreens. In seconds we both were deep in a whispering game of being Finnish ski troopers on a dangerous mission. Packing our gear quietly, we secretively slid to the trail and set off to give our imagined pursuers the slip. And then we both began laughing, amused with our childishness but happy about it as well. Grown-ups need fun, too. And now whenever we meet we remember the incident and chuckle with pleasure. Have fun ski touring; there is nothing wrong with that. And it's good for the head.

Reading about cross-country is another way to enjoy your sport. Of course, it is instructive as well. There is a near-blizzard of "how-to" books on the shelves these days. The big ski magazines also are regularly offering more and more pages on touring. Usually this is a mixture of "how-to" copy and pictures and articles on back-country tours or mountaineering trips that offer a variety of guidance, lessons, and warnings. If it has been a hard day of business, there is a special pleasure in sitting by a fireside in the evening and reading about your favorite sport.

Another profitable experience for body and mind is to arrange for a day or half-day ski-touring lesson with a qualified instructor. It would be pretty hard today to find a ski area in the Rockies that does not have one or more top-notch cross-country ski schools or individual instructors. With their help it is easy to add a bit of new technique or to straighten out a problem that might have crept into your style. The biggest challenge they can help you with is improving your Nordic downhill technique. It is possible to parallel or short-swing on cross-country skis, even with a pack on your back, but it

Heading for a ridgeline, this cross-country skier step-climbs and traverses. *David Summer*

certainly cuts down the learning time if you have a good instructor to follow.

When we explore the cross-country possibilities at the downhill ski areas that are spread throughout the four-state region, we will also list the many ski-touring schools and cross-country instructors who work in and around them.

Eating on the trail

One sure way to take care of a ski tourer's head is through his stomach. And, as a general rule, the tour party that is quickly fed at a food break will consider itself well fed. With just a little planning and a stop at a supermarket, it is quite simple to put together the food and drink you will need for a lunch or an all-day ski tour. Food planning and preparation for overnight and longer trips requires quite a bit more work. But first let's look at some general rules for food on the ski trail.

The food you pack along should be compact, easily digested, high in energy and in body-building protein. It should meet the following three basic requirements: portability (lots of food value without bulk); storability (nonspoiling even without cooling); and it should be easily prepared (reduced cooking time and increased rest time).

When it comes to a lunch or day hike, these rules are met easily. You are certain to have everybody's favorites if you pack along sufficient amounts of good cheeses, cold meats, dark bread, wine and fruit drinks, water, oranges, cookies, and a mixed bag of small candy bars. You also may buy or prepare some "gorp," a ready-to-eat, high-energy mixture of dried fruits, nuts, seeds, and whatever else in bite-sized pieces appeals to you. Put it in a plastic bag and keep it in an outside pack pocket so that you or your companions can grab a handful at a wax or rest break. Packing along some dextrose tablets also is recommended should a tourer begin to lag and need a quick shot of energy.

If you are going to be out all day, it's not a bad idea to plan a hot drink break in the middle of the afternoon when it is beginning to cool and fatigue is rising. Building a small fire

Honest appetite and thirst give these ski tourers, on the hike up Homestake Creek near Vail, the pleasure of food and drink at their fullest. *Susan Biddle*

may take too much time, so plan to pack along a lightweight propane or butane stove. A cup of hot bouillon and a handful of gorp will perk the party right up. The final glide back to the trail head will be enjoyed just as much as the run out.

When you are planning an overnight or longer back-country trip, it is well to start by making a list of everything you will want in terms of food. This will assure that you plan your menus carefully and completely, and it will give you a shopping and packing checkoff list.

There are any number of good books dealing with menus for outdoor, Alpine cooking. A bit of study and selection from them is highly recommended before planning a ski-touring trip of more than a day. Again, what you'll be seeking is food that is compact but provides a well-rounded diet. In addition to tasting good, you will want to be sure that your menus provide sufficient amounts of vitamins, roughage, protein, carbohydrates (energy from food sugars), and water and salt to keep the body from becoming dehydrated.

On the trail or in an evening camp it is easiest to boil, broil, or pan fry food. A fine approach is to pre-mix and pre-pack so that everything can be plopped at one time into the pot or pan for a quick and satisfying hot meal. Mountaineering and back-country outfitting shops offer a wide range of freeze-dried foods and mixed meals. These generally are excellent if a bit expensive. With the addition of boiling water, a few ounces of freeze-dried food can turn into a heaping plate of dinner. Another and cheaper place to shop is among the dehydrated foods in your supermarket. Soups and meals of all kinds may be found there. Before throwing away the excess packaging that most of these foods are sold in, be sure to read the preparation instructions, and take them along if necessary.

A well-fed ski touring party is happier—and far safer.

Part of the back-country ethic is that what you pack in you pack out. There are, of course, some reasonable exceptions. If you have an open fire, disposing of burnable debris will cut down your firewood demand as well as reduce your load. Birds, such as camp robbers, and some ground animals might attend your luncheon festivities. If they will eat food scraps, let them be your guests. But leave your campsite clean when you go. Also, if you must relieve yourself during a day tour, get well away from the trail or water course. Your advance planning should assure that you have a substantial supply of toilet paper as well as a closeable plastic bag in which to carry the soiled paper out of the woods.

First Aid

One sure component of mental peace and comfort that you can provide for yourself and others ski touring with you is a confident knowledge of first aid. You don't have to be ski-patrol or emergency-crew caliber, although that wouldn't hurt. The local Red Cross chapter in most cities regularly sponsors training courses. And if you live in a ski mountain area, the patrol usually conducts a refresher course in the fall that any interested person can attend. When you go off ski touring, carry along your first-aid manual as well as a simple kit of self-stick bandages, Mercurochrome, first-aid cream, aspirin, and any other items that strike your fancy, such as an ace bandage.

Your first-aid preparations for a day tour can cover only minor injuries—generally the type you meet in ski touring—and the prevention of shock should someone be seriously hurt. In all likelihood you will need ski patrol help to get a seriously injured person out of the woods. The prescription for that situation is to send the best skier or two back to the trail head for help while the injured skier is kept warm and quiet and given liquids as necessary to prevent shock.

A serious physical injury—rare in cross-country skiing—unfortunately does happen. And then you must depend upon your first-aid training, pre-planning, and quiet good sense. But there is another type of ski-touring injury that should never happen. It occurs because of bad planning, foolishness, and panic. In the High Country environment this type of "injury" can be deadly. We will take a look at the High Country and its dangers in the next chapter.

3—The High Country Environment

Venturing into the High Country of the Rocky Mountains in wintertime is a special type of adventure that no true outdoors person should miss. There is an awesome grandeur to the rugged scenery whether it be deep forest slopes, high craggy mountains, narrow Alpine valleys, or the broad "parks" that lie between the ranges. Traveling through this winter country under your own steam on touring skis, preserving the quiet and the country, has to be the best way to visit it.

Though a world of great beauty, it also harbors very special dangers. There are traps for the unwary, threats to the mountaineer, and hazards for ski tourers moving any distance away from the resources of developed areas. These dangers can be met, however, so that your relationship to the high winter mountains may focus on the beauty of good feelings they provide rather than on the hazards they naturally hold. The tools for meeting these dangers are knowledge, experience, and careful planning.

Much of the knowledge you will need may be gleaned from a large and steadily growing literature on winter backpacking and ski mountaineering. Ski magazines have been expanding their coverage of ski touring. From these articles you may pick up many how-to and how-not-to hints from the ski trip experiences of others. Forest Service pamphlets on winter recreation and safety are available for the asking, and forest rangers working in the areas where you plan to ski tour will be glad to discuss the country with you and share their special knowledge of it. The final and best knowledge will be what you gain on your own as you go touring with experienced local skiers or a trained mountain ski-touring guide.

This education will give you the confidence to be out in the Rocky Mountain winter world as a member or leader of a ski-touring party. You will come to understand the threat of such hazards as hypothermia and avalanche and how to reduce them to a minimum. You will become alert to weather changes and understand what they forecast. You will learn to carry all the necessary gear and supplies for comfort and safety. You will be prepared to provide first aid or respond to the unexpected. And, finally, you will know where you are, where you are going, and about how long it will take you to get there.

Altitude

When you go suddenly from the lowlands to the High Country, you are almost sure to suffer some of the effects of altitude or mountain sickness. People vary considerably in their response to altitude and the time needed to acclimatize based on their general physical condition and other less understood factors. But almost everyone early on will suffer some shortness of breath and a related light-headedness, particularly when exerting. Other common symptoms are headache and difficulty in sleeping the first night or two. Smoking and drinking alcohol also will have an affect on how well and how quickly you adjust to higher elevations. Most healthy people adjust rapidly to the thin air and in a few days will be able to perform to their maximum. Drinking extra water seems to help this adjustment. But a few people suffer severely as they reach higher and higher elevations. Symptoms include vomiting, violent headache, and a growing dizzyness that can lead to unconsciousness. If you feel severe illness coming on or see it developing in another in the party, the only answer is to turn back and head for a lower altitude.

Let's take a moment to talk about turning back. The reversal, of course, it must be stressed, is the one essential maneuver designed to get you out of trouble before you get into it. Ego or machismo must have no bearing on the decision to execute a 180-degree turn and head for safety. Experienced pilots and mountain travelers are experienced just because they have had the good sense over the years to spot the obvious and not-so-obvious warning signs of danger and make that turn. You too can learn the warning signs. Know that you are in good company when you sensibly announce, "We're turning back."

The breathtaking splendor of evergreens and white snow blankets surround ski tourers at the Devil's Thumb Cross-Country Ski Center in Fraser, Colorado. *Sidney Fingerman/Devil's Thumb Cross-Country Ski Center*

Weather

Winter weather in the High Country of the Rockies is reasonably predictable as storm systems come blowing in off the Pacific and work their way eastward. Wetter snows will be dumped on the Cascades and Sierras. Dryer snows will fall on the ranges in Utah, Colorado, Arizona, and New Mexico. But now and then warmer, wet air systems can curl up from the south to shower the Rockies in heavy, wet snow, just as biting cold Arctic fronts can storm down from Canada.

On the average, though, there are reasonably regular seasons within the winter season. Blustery snow storms, which run for days, and spells of biting, clear cold generally mark the first part of the winter season. By mid-January there are substantial periods of better weather and even the possibility of a mild thaw. The well-advertised Rocky Mountain weather of sun in the day and powder snow at night really gets going in February and can run on through spring. However, heavy storms are likely at any time, and they can be particularly severe and marked by heightened avalanche danger as the snow season gets into late March and April.

There have been years in the Rockies when it seemed to snow steadily all winter and others when it seemed hardly to snow at all. But if you are looking for generally sunshiny days mixed with pleasant falls of a few inches of light powder, late winter and early spring in the Rockies are a fairly safe bet. This sort of weather information, however, just lets you plan a general time for your Nordic ski visit. The weather that most concerns you is the day-to-day and even hour-to-hour weather that you will encounter.

Just about anyone can become a rule-of-thumb meteorologist. A simple understanding of weather systems will provide a substantial safety factor in your ski touring. It will be particularly effective if you tend to err—and everybody guesses wrong about the weather—on the side of caution.

Old farmers, old salts, and old mountaineers perhaps knew little about highs and lows and the circulation of air about them. But they did know from years of observation that when the wind shifted in a certain way or the temperature changed suddenly or certain types of clouds began filling the sky, reasonably predictable weather changes were going to occur within a certain time span. You also may use the tool of your own observations. Your learning curve, however, can be speeded up by reading about weather systems and local air movements in any number of good outdoor books. Then you will know with fair certainty that a particular wind shift during a multi-day back-country trip heralds the arrival of a bad-weather low system or a good-weather high.

One weather effect of special concern to ski tourers is that caused by temperature changes at the surface of the snow. The character of the top few inches of snow responds to temperature changes of only a few degrees. As the temperature climbs during the day, the snow will get softer and wetter and require softer waxes to allow you to travel. But with the cooling of late afternoon, the surface will start to freeze, and a re-waxing will be required to give you kick or let you climb. These surface snow variations can be encountered, sometimes startlingly, when you move from a slope facing the sun to one facing away and vice versa. Similar surprises might occur when you move from open meadow to deep forest. A couple of sudden spills from sharp acceleration or deceleration will commence your education about the local snow effects of temperature variations.

Another daily weather pattern of interest to ski tourers who are out on an overnight or longer trip is the surface movement of air (local wind) based on variations in the sun's heating of the earth. During the day, as valleys and basins warm up, the air above them will heat and start to rise, creating an uphill wind. This wind usually will develop and strengthen during the day if the sun stays out. But when the sun drops, the higher, cooler air will start to slide back down the mountains to fill the valleys. As evening turns to night, the lowest parts of the valley or basin can become much colder than a few hundred feet higher up the slope. Remember this temperature shift when you select a campsite. With a little elevation above the valley floor you could be a lot more comfortable overnight, and you might awaken in the early sun to see a cold, moist cloud down below you. It also is wise to remember this wind shift if you are planning to have an open campfire. Place your tent and resting area where the evening downhill wind won't blow smoke right into your eyes.

Avalanche

Winter weather and western mountain terrain combine to produce the very real and very serious hazard of avalanche. You are not under constant threat every time you pin on your bindings and set forth. With a little planning, you generally can lunch-hike or day-tour through areas that have little or no avalanche danger. But if you plan to range away from established trails for a day or take overnight or longer back-country trips, you had best be prepared to deal with potential or actual avalanche conditions.

Study and observation soon will have you briefed on the basic types of avalanches and the weather and terrain factors that create them. No matter the type of avalanche or whether it is large or small, they can all pack tremendous force and pose a serious threat to the life of anyone caught by them. By exercising caution and detouring around the most obvious hazard areas, you can reduce your risk greatly. But if a skier is caught by an avalanche, earlier precautions and proper rescue techniques can greatly improve the victim's chances of coming out alive.

The two principal types of avalanches are loose snow and slab. A loose snow avalanche is triggered by some mechanical event—heavy snow clumps blown from a tree, a wind-created

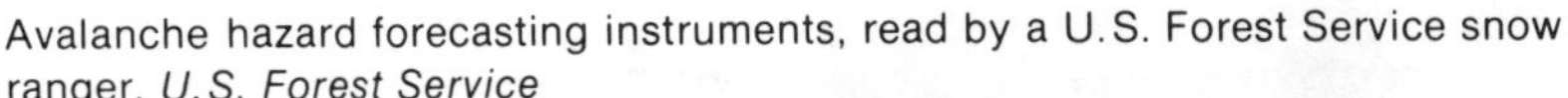

Avalanche hazard forecasting instruments, read by a U.S. Forest Service snow ranger. *U.S. Forest Service*

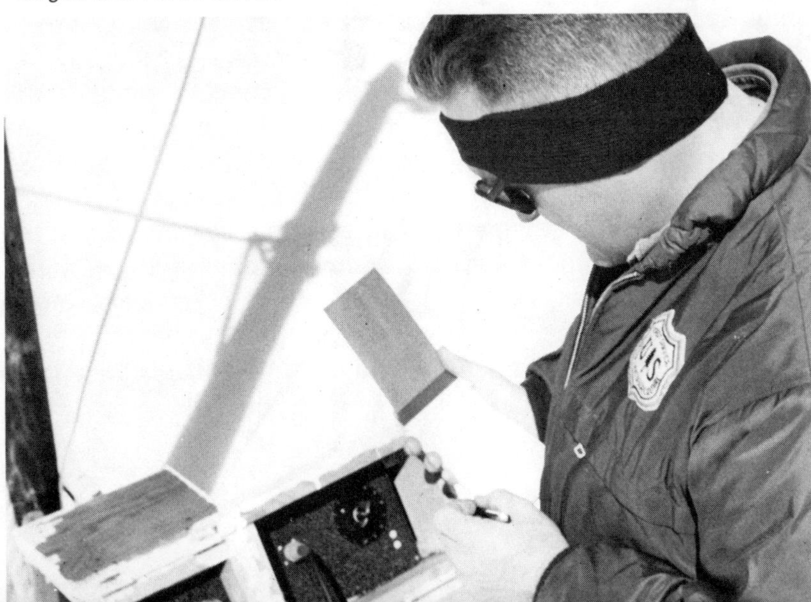

cornice collapsing—affecting a point on a slope that usually is between 30 and 45 degrees. Avalanches, however, can occur on slopes of as little as 15 degrees to as great as 65 degrees. The new, loose snow starts sliding on the older, more compacted layer beneath it and quickly grows in size and quantity as it descends until it reaches an area level and wide enough to stop its progress and hold its weight. There is little internal cohesion to such a slide; it is just a great rolling mass of loose snow setting every other bit of loose snow in its path moving downhill.

Though unquestionably dangerous, particularly if the snow is wet and will set up hard when it comes to rest, you have a better chance with this type than with the other: a slab avalanche. Slab avalanches occur in older, more settled snow where some cohesion has developed. An entire mass of snow begins to move at once, separating from more stable snow

Notice the heavy, wet snow clinging to very steep surfaces in Colorado. This is a likely spot for an avalanche to begin. *U.S. Forest Service*

above it at a fracture line. Its own weight or rising temperature can snap the tenuous bond holding it to an underlying
snow layer or the ground. Another unfortunate trigger can be
the passage of a skier cutting the surface crust at a point of
great tension at the top or bottom of the slab. These slabs tend
to break into large blocks as they slide and crash into one
another before they come to rest, stacking up the way they slid
down the mountain. If a skier is caught in a slab avalanche,
remember where he was on the slab when it began to move.
You will have a better idea of where in the pile to begin your
search.

Avalanches tend to occur again and again in the same
areas, so keep a sharp eye out for the signs of avalanche
paths. Indicators of earlier avalanche activity are a stretch of
trees with their lower limbs broken off or a number of fallen
small trees. Be particularly wary on open slopes and in steep

Avalanche busting by using a 75mm shell in the Wasatch National Forest, Utah. *U.S. Forest Service*

gullies. Also watch the ridgeline above and ahead of you as you travel for cornices or wind-blown plumes of snow. Moving below or onto cornices is simply foolhardy; they can give way at any moment. Snow plumes from ridges and peaks show snow moving onto lee slopes, creating potentially threatening conditions.

A good safety caution is the old railroad crossing sign: "Stop, Look, Listen." Take the time to look around you, noting recent avalanche activity near you or on far slopes. Also look for old slide paths, cracks in the snow, and snowballs that have rolled or are rolling down the slope. If it is snowing, observe the kind of crystals that are falling. Small needle and pellet crystals produce more dangerous conditions than the familiar star-shaped snowflake. Your ears can give you warning also. You may hear avalanche activity that you cannot see. And if the snow on the slope you are crossing sounds hollow, particularly on a leeward slope, it indicates unstable snow inside the pack. Should the snow surface crack and the cracks propagate, slab avalanche danger is high. Clear out fast.

Most avalanches occur during or shortly after heavy snowfalls or windstorms. (If snow falls at the rate of an inch or more an hour, the danger of avalanche increases rapidly.) When caught in such a storm, it is a good idea to wait it out in a safe camp (or take a known safe route out) for at least a day after the storm ends. You can find plenty to do by sharpening your mountain and survival skills with snow-cave or igloo building, a try at gourmet trail cooking, or just observing the woods in winter. And what's the rush, anyway? Back-country skiing or ski mountaineering are not travel modes designed to move you rapidly from point A to point B.

Picking a safe route is the best precaution against avalanche danger. The windward side of ridgelines, well back from cornices, is the safest route. The next safest route is out in the valley well clear of the slope bottoms. When the valley bottom is sharp, try to determine which slope is leeward of the prevailing wind, and move up a safe distance from the bottom on the windward slope. When climbing or descending, try to travel along spur ridges, in the heavier timber, or along a line

A dry slab avalanche in the Wasatch National Forest, Utah, caused by artillery release. *U.S. National Park Service*

protected by rock outcroppings. If you must go up or down an open and potentially dangerous slope, try to go straight up and and down. Traverse as little as possible; do not go back and forth across the slope.

Another basic and inviolable rule is that only one person at a time should cross a dangerous slope with the rest of the party watching. Just because the first person gets across safely, is no sign that the slope is safe. An avalanche can move at anytime, catching the first or last or middle man or anyone in between. Before crossing the slope it is imperative that you be ready to rid yourself of all equipment if you should kick off or be picked up in an avalanche. Remove your ski poles from around your wrists, take off your ski safety straps and set the bindings as loose as possible, sling your pack over one shoulder, and loosen other equipment so that you can discard it quickly.

You also want to close up all your clothing, pulling your cap down and your hood over your head with drawstring snugged. If caught, you don't want snow inside your clothing. Do not forget to put your mittens on. Also release and trail behind you your brightly colored nylon avalanche line. It literally could be your lifeline. Then cross the danger area near the top and at a swift downward angle. You'll get across faster, and you are less likely to trigger a fracture.

If the worst happens and you are caught in an avalanche, immediately try to get rid of all your equipment, including your skis. With luck and set loosely, they might be wrenched off you. Make swimming motions to try to stay on top of the slide while working your way to the side. When you feel the snow coming to a stop, cover your mouth and nose with one hand while clearing out as large a space in front of your face as you can. Then see if you can push an arm straight up out of the slide. If your sense of direction has been confused and not enough light is coming through the snow to indicate up, spit easily into the space in front of you. If the saliva falls back on you, you are facing up. If it falls on your hands, which should be out in front of your face, you will have the opposite directional clue. Digging your own way out might be possible if the grip of the snow is not too strong. But work calmly, maintaining your air space. If stuck, try to remain calm. Help from your group is on the way. Do not waste your strength calling out since snow just soaks up sound.

Should one of your party be caught in an avalanche, mentally note and then mark, with a pack, a jacket, or a hat, the spot where you last saw him, and immediately begin your search downslope from that point. Look for the victim's avalanche cord or pieces of equipment or clothing. If the victim is not visible at the surface of the slide, scuff it and probe it as you move down with an inverted ski pole, a stick, or the tail of a ski. A body under the snow will give dull resistance to the probe. Immediate rescue is the victim's best hope for survival; after being buried for 30 minutes, his survival chances are only 50 percent. So send a member of your party off for help only if it is nearby and there are others to help you conduct a probe of the slide.

If there are no surface clues as to the victim's whereabouts, you will have to start an uphill, coarse probe, beginning at the most likely point at the bottom of the slide to which the victim would have been carried. You will find the details of coarse- and fine-probe searching in your mountaineering books. But remember to search with special care near obstructions in the slide line such as tree trunks or large rocks where the victim might have been stopped. And when you find him, administer first aid and treat for suffocation and shock.

Other Threats

There are other cold-weather threats facing those who venture into the back country. Hypothermia and frostbite are two, with hypothermia (commonly called "exposure") the number one killer of outdoorsmen. It involves a lowering of the body's temperature that leads to mental and physical collapse. Exposure to cold, which does not have to be freezing or below, is the essential condition. A wind-chill factor, wet clothing, and exhaustion aggravate the effects of the cold, and the body begins to lose heat faster than it can produce it. At this point the victim is suffering from exposure; what is necessary to halt and reverse the body's cooling trend must be done immediately. If it isn't, the cold finally will reach the brain, numbing reasoning power, and body control will fail. This is hypothermia; only external assistance at this point can prevent collapse and death.

Before heading into the back country—even for just a day trip—it would be well to brief yourself once again on the cause and treatment of hypothermia, frostbite, altitude sickness, dehydration, hyperventilation, and any other threat that accident or inattention to safety precautions can visit upon your ski party. A quick and handy review may be found in the Forest Service's "Winter Recreation Safety Guide," which was prepared in cooperation with the U.S. Ski Association. Pick up a copy and keep it in your pack.

U.S. Park Service rangers with rescue equipment, ready to move out in Rocky Mountain National Park, Colorado. *U.S. National Park Service*

Also before setting forth on anything from a lunch hike to a long sojourn in the back country, you should make or check a previously made list of things you must have with you. Obviously, the character of your trip will determine a number of the things you will or will not take, but there are certain essentials that should be with you at all times unless you are just out for a slide around the local golf course.

Proper clothing and equipment in good shape are the most obvious requirements. First-aid needs should have your attention; do not forget a manual. A repair kit, consisting of knife, screwdriver, wire, tape, and extra ski tip, is mandatory. If waxing, check that you have plenty of wax and all of the other items needed to clean and re-wax your skis. A map, compass, and flashlight are essential if you are planning to leave a well-known, beaten path. Consider your water, food, and fire needs. packing along a light, winter stove if that seems necessary. Finally, check off extra clothing and shelter requirements that might be needed due to a weather change or accident.

If you do this systematically and err on the side of caution, you should never find yourself deep in snow and far from help, wishing there were a supermarket or mountaineering store over the next rise.

4 — Maps and Compass

There are many ways of getting lost when traveling in the back country of the Rockies or, for that matter, anywhere else where comfortable street signs and highway markers are absent. It can happen in the summer but not as easily or as dangerously as in the winter. The principal reasons for getting lost are thoughtlessness, lack of observation, faulty or insufficient planning, and brave, bold ignorance.

Anyone can become temporarily disoriented. Apparent shortcuts that don't work out, unexpected terrain formations causing detours, sudden weather changes, or a period of simple doping off because the country is so beautiful might suddenly leave you wondering if you know where you are. Nobody likes to admit to being lost. But if you have the slightest nervous doubt as to your whereabouts, stop and figure it out.

For all the ways of getting lost there are at least an equal number of ways not to get lost, to find your location and line of travel. (And if you really cannot find out where you are, there are things to do to let others find you.) The first defense against getting seriously lost is common sense, panic's enemy.

It will do as much or more for you than a directional sixth sense, which is really just experience by another name. Next are the two essentials of back-country travel: a proper map and compass and the knowledge of how to use them. These tools supplement your general observations of your starting point, your general line of travel, and how fast and how far you have traveled. Other indications such as the line of the ranges and the run of the drainages also help to keep you safe and "found."

This chapter is not intended to be a complete guide to the use of map and compass. But a once-over-lightly review will assure that you are on the right course when it comes to "orienteering" yourself in the Rocky Mountain High Country. Orienteering has been defined as the game of taking yourself from point to point, using map and compass. If you play it well, it will remain a game. If you play it poorly, you might suddenly find yourself in peril.

Maps

When you begin planning a ski-touring trip into the back country of the Rocky Mountains, you should collect a variety of maps from which to glean important information. State road maps put out by the oil companies (or similar maps produced by map companies) let you familiarize yourself with the major features of roads and settlements in the area where you plan to ski tour. If your trip will take you onto U.S. Park Service or Forest Service land (and that's a good bet since most of the High Country ski-touring land belongs to the federal government), contact the Forest or Park office and ask for their visitor's map. (We will give you some addresses further on.) You may be asked to pay 50¢; the maps are well worth it. They show forest boundaries, and name forests, ranger stations and campgrounds, towns and villages on the edge of the forests, and lakes, rivers, creeks, and the number or name of trails, roads, and highways.

These maps are very helpful in the general planning of your trip—places to park and sources of supply or assistance—

but they do not give you the terrain information, the topography, that you really need. For that you will need the U.S. Geological Survey 7.5-minute-series maps. These maps are the ones to use for detailed trip plotting. They should go along with you and your compass into the back country. Their presentation of contoured terrain information will let you plan and navigate with confidence.

When you know in which state or states of the four discussed in this book you plan to ski tour in, contact the U.S. Geological Survey at the Federal Center, Building 41, Denver, Colorado 80225. Ask them for the index of topographical maps for Colorado, Utah, New Mexico, or Arizona. It's free. You will find each state cross-hatched with a grid of lines that mark off boxes representing 7.5 minutes of latitude and longitude. Each of the quadrangles has a name, which usually is taken from the most prominent land feature or a town shown on the map.

These maps are drawn to a scale of 1:24,000. In the bottom margin there are scale measures for miles, feet, and kilometers. With a pair of dividers or the edge of a piece of paper with the appropriate marks transferred to it, you can measure off the horizontal distance between points on the map. If you plan to travel along the line you are measuring, don't forget to allow for the vertical distance as shown by the contour lines. The scale represented by these fine brown lines can vary from map to map, depending upon the character of the terrain in the area. The contour interval is stated in the bottom margin of each map. At a regular interval there will be a heavier brown line. Follow along it and you will find the elevation above sealevel for that line. Then, to find the elevation of a point between that heavy line and the next, just add or subtract the proper value for the number of fine brown contour lines you cross.

By noting how the contour lines close up or space out along the line of your proposed travel you will be able to visualize the terrain. Whether it will be an up or down slope for you depends on the direction of your travel. You may quickly determine that by noting whether the numbers on the heavier brown lines are increasing or decreasing. If you wish to know more exactly how steep a particular slope is, measure the horizontal feet it covers and divide that number into the vertical feet shown by the contour lines. For example, if the horizontal distance measures 1,000 feet and the vertical distance 1,000 feet, you have what is called a 100 percent slope. For every horizontal foot you cover, you will climb one foot; the slope is rising—or falling—at 45 degrees. If the horizontal distance were 1,000 feet but the vertical rise only 500 feet, you would be on a 50 percent slope. For every 2 horizontal feet covered, you would rise or drop one foot. You can get some appreciation for the steepness of a slope for which you have worked out a percentage by noting that the steepest grade allowed on a mountain road is 12 percent. That is, for every 8-plus feet traveled horizontally, you climb or drop one foot.

The 7.5-minute maps show Jeep trails and pack and foot trails along with other man-made features. Though these trails might provide you with a good line of travel, don't plan to follow them slavishly in the winter without carefully examining how they cut across the terrain. A foot trail that is perfectly safe in summer might slice across a leeward slope or halfway up a gully. That's no place for you in winter. With your "topo" map you can plot the safest route over the snow for your cross-country skiing party.

Map and Compass

To use a map for determining a compass line of travel when out in the woods, you first need to orient the map. That is, the map should be positioned so it is lined up accurately with the terrain. The top of the map, which always is north, must face in that direction. You can roughly position your map by aligning it with a few prominent landmarks. To fine-tune it into position, use your compass.

Once the map is oriented, you can determine your position on it either by your proximity to a distinct feature or, better, by sighting lines to terrain features and noting where they intersect. Depending upon your needs, you may either pinpoint or just roughly spot your position.

One style of orienting compass used for cross-country travel. *U.S. National Park Service*

For cross-country travel there are two ways to use your compass. One is in conjunction with your map, the other by compass alone. If you can see your destination or a known prominent point along your line of travel, simply sight across your compass to the feature and then follow that reading through woods and terrain that block you from it for a time. Remember when you sight to line up the north end of the magnetic needle with the north mark on the movable rim of the compass. Sighting directly across the compass to the landmark will give you a heading in relation to magnetic north. That is all you need to know; just follow the degree reading from one terrain feature to the next as you head for your destination.

There are any number of reasons, however, why you might want to work out a compass heading to be followed for a trip from A to B on a particular map. Some of them are:

1. You cannot see the destination for lack of landmarks or distance.
2. You cannot see the destination because of poor weather.
3. You are half a continent away planning the trip, and so on.

By understanding how your compass works and how your map is drawn, you can establish the proper magnetic north heading from points A to B, just as though you were running a line-of-sight.

Let's discuss the way maps are drawn and how compasses work, how the two differ, and how they relate. Once you understand the principles, working up a technique to use them together is no problem at all.

The grid lines on your map, lines of latitude and longitude, and the section lines drawn parallel to them, are drawn in relationship to the geographical North Pole, or true north. Your compass, however, the other tool you must use for map and compass travel, points to the magnetic North Pole. That pole is slightly northwest of Hudson Bay. Only along one line of longitude will your magnetic compass needle also point to true north. As you move away from that line, angle will develop, either to the east or the west, between your compass reading

Type 15 orienting compass (right), the "Ranger." *(Silva Company)*

The type 4W wrist compass (below), particularly suited for the cross-country skier and canoeist. *(Silva Company)*

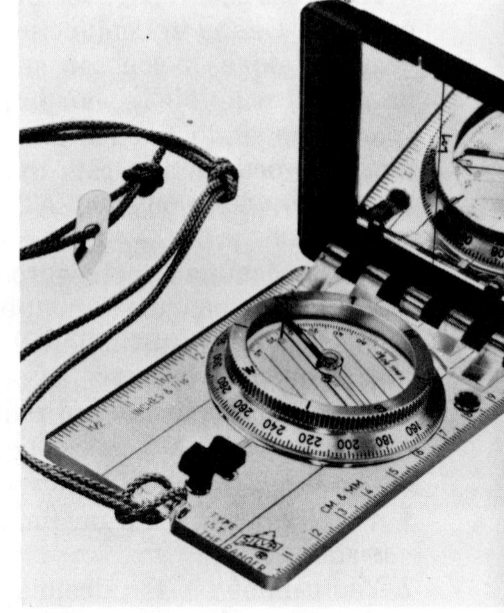

of north and true north. This is called declination. It varies based on your geographical position. Most good maps, such as your U.S. Geological Survey topographical maps, tell you what the declination, the difference between true and magnetic north, is for that particular piece of country.

Let's start with the goal since there are a number of ways to get to it. What you wish to achieve when traveling by compass is to get from point A to point B by following a compass heading that matches the line of travel when the magnetic compass needle is pointing to the north indicator on the movable compass ring. The ring, or perhaps the entire compass housing, must be moved to bring the north mark in line with the north-pointing end of the needle. The magnetic needle is the fixed element—everything else must be adjusted to it. Of course, you can confound the needle by having a steel beer can in one hand as you try to make readings, but then you deserve your trouble. Get away from your car also.

Once you have the needle and the north mark on the compass ring or compass housing aligned, you are ready to make readings that will determine your line of travel. As you can see, you have established a fixed relationship between the magnetic north-pointing needle and the north indicator on the movable 360-degree circle or housing that surrounds it. To walk a straight line in any direction, all you have to do is pick your line of travel, or heading, and follow it while maintaining the fixed relationship between the north end of the compass needle and the north indicator on the compass ring. But how do you do that when you want to follow a line on a map that is drawn in relation to true north? Quite simply. Here we go.

There are a variety of compasses, from old army types to new "orienteering" devices and any number in between. The basic principles for using them do not change, however. If you understand them, you will be able to use any compass with any map as long as you know what the magnetic north heading, the declination, is for the area the map covers.

If you are in the field, the first step is to orient your map to the terrain. Use two or more prominent, separated, "sharp" landmarks or, better, your compass. To orient the map using your compass, first lay the map out flat with its top pointed in the general direction of north. Next, place your compass on one of the north-south grid lines so that the line bisects the compass.

Rotate the compass rim that bears the degree markings until the "N" for north lines up with the north end of the compass needle. Now, without moving the compass, rotate the map under it so that the bisected grid line is aligned with the compass needle, with the north end of the needle pointing toward the top of the map. Now you must determine what the magnetic north declination is for your map. Some maps print it in

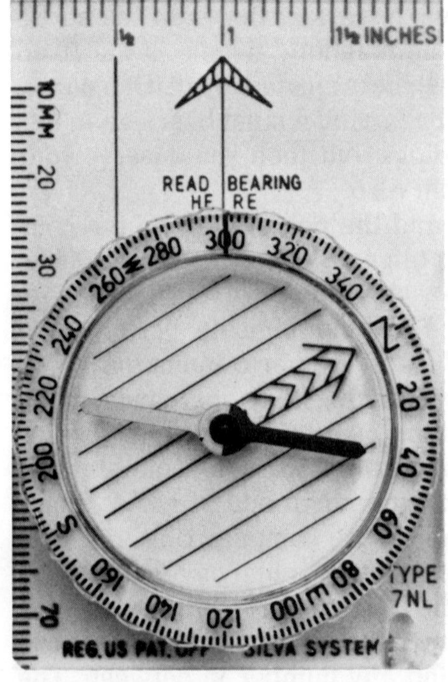

Type 7 compass, "Polaris." *(Silva Company)*

a note, others might have a little arrow diagram at the bottom. The reason we need to know the declination is because your compass is pointing to magnetic north while the grid lines are drawn to true north. To align the map accurately with the terrain, it is necessary to adjust for this difference.

For the purposes of this exercise, we will consider two cases. In the first, we will assume a magnetic north declination of 10 degrees west. In the second, we will look at 10 degrees east. What you need to know and remember is that a declination to the west is *added* and a declination to the east is *subtracted.* To help you remember, learn the rhyme "West is best (add), East is least (subtract)."

To orient the map to our 10-degree-west declination, rotate it, without disturbing the compass, so that the north-south grid line bisects the compass at 10 degrees. We have added 10 degrees; the map is oriented to the terrain. If we now draw an A to B line on the map and position our compass over it so that it bisects the compass while keeping the needle on the north heading indicator, we can read the line-of-travel bearing at the point where the A-B line meets the compass rim.

Our second declination example is 10 degrees east. We want to subtract that amount. Again, starting with the needle aligned to a north-south grid line, we rotate the map under the compass until the grid line we are bisecting runs through the compass rim at 350 degrees. The map now is aligned properly to the terrain.

A quick way to orient your map if it has a true north-magnetic north diagram of arrows along its bottom margin is to align your compass needle with the magnetic north arrow.

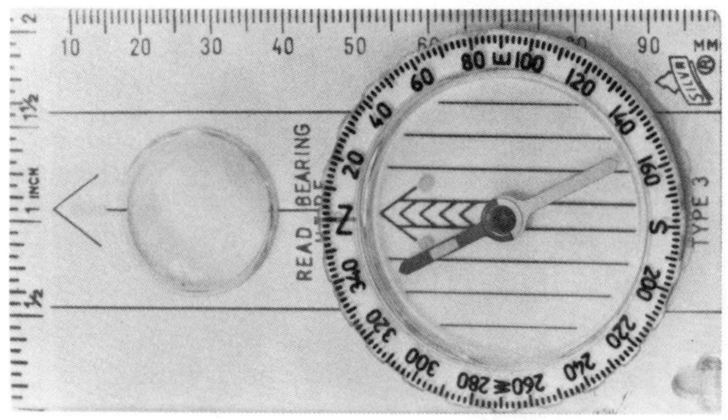

Type 3 compass, "Explorer." *(Silva Company)*

That arrow represents the declination for the map. Then, without disturbing map or compass, rotate the compass rim until the "N" lines up with the north end of the needle. Once again, the map is aligned, and you are ready to read the magnetic heading of a line of travel from A to B.

To find the heading from B to A, simply add or subtract 180

degrees, depending upon whether your original heading is larger or smaller than 180 degrees.

Should you happen to be sitting back in your living room a thousand miles from the Rockies, you still can determine the magnetic heading of a planned course. But now you will need a 360-degree protractor since your compass will be indicating the local declination, not the declination of the map. First draw your course line. Then pinpoint the center of your protractor over the point made where your line of travel bisects a north-south grid line on the map. (If for any reason your point-to-point line is so short that it doesn't cross a north-south grid line, just extend it until it does.) Rotate the protractor until the 0- or 360-degree mark and the 180-degree mark fall on the north-south line, with the 360-degree mark pointed to the top of the map.

You now have a true north reading for your line of travel. But that won't do you much good when you are actually there, using your compass, which points to magnetic north. What you must do is find the declination for the map. Say it is 10

Type 23 compass, the "Huntsman," is a pin-on model that leaves both hands free. *(Silva Company)*

degrees west. If you rotate your protractor counterclockwise, keeping its center on the point where the north-south grid line and your line of travel bisect, until you reach 10 degrees (add because the declination is west), you can read the magnetic heading for your planned line of travel. Let's assume that the true north heading of your line of travel was 80 degrees. With the addition of the map's declination of 10 degrees west, you now will have a line-of-travel heading of 90 degrees. You might wish to write along the line, in the direction of your travel, "C 090 Mag."

The "C" stands for compass, the numbers for the line-of-travel compass bearing, and the "Mag" for magnetic. Even though all your bearings will in all likelihood be magnetic, it is just as well to indicate that they are in case someone else has to use the map you have marked. And they can feel comfortable that you have made allowance for declination.

It is strongly recommended that you obtain any one of a number of good books on the use of map and compass, as well as an orienting-type compass. One highly regarded book is *Be Expert with Map and Compass* by Bjorn Kjellstrom, published in 1967 by American Orienting Service, La Porte, Indiana. There are a variety of compasses that incorporate a line-of-travel sighting device. One very simple and effective orienting compass is the Silva System. It consists of a magnetic needle, a revolving dial marked with the points of the compass, and a transparent base plate marked with a line-of-travel arrow.

With these tools and a map for your area, you can practice a range of travel-by-compass problems. You will learn how to work around obstacles in your direct line of travel so that you come back to your original heading. You can practice the art of finding yourself from compass bearings when "lost." All this safe, weekend practice in and around your home base will mean safety for you and your ski-touring party when high up in the Rockies.

Trail Markings

Whenever you get away from ski-touring practice trails in and around the downhill ski areas in the West, you are more than likely to be on U.S. Forest Service land. Your back-country or ski-mountaineering trips might be almost wholly in the national forests. For that reason it is well to be familiar with the marks the U.S. Forest Service uses to blaze its trails. As was noted earlier, there will be stretches of Forest Service trails that you won't or can't follow in winter as they cut across a lee slope. But many trails, particularly those in deep woods, might make your snow travels much easier, provided the trail was clear of jackpiles of downed timber when the snows came in late fall.

In all likelihood the trail signs, naming the trails and giving the miles to particular terrain features such as a lake or lookout point, that are to be found in summer at points along the trail will be buried in deep snow. The worn track of the trail obviously will not be visible either. But there are other trail

On tour from Vail Pass over Shrine Pass down to the town of Red Cliff, Colorado.
Susan Biddle

markings that can help you. These are blazes well up on tree trunks, with the marked trees generally in line-of-sight of one another. The blaze may be the scar left by axing off the bark in a vertical long and short dash or a splotch of bright spray paint. By working with your map, which will have the trail indicated on it, and taking a compass bearing on a landmark or two, you should find it relatively simple to locate your approximate position and to determine your rate of travel point-to-point.

However, because trees fall down now and then or other unplanned acts occur, the sequence of blazed trees may be broken for a stretch. Quite often the line of the trail is reasonably obvious from the lay of the land or by a bit of map study. Soon enough you will pick up another blaze. But if you should become really puzzled as to the whereabouts of the "lost" trail and feel lost without it, there are two things to do. First, stop thrashing on. Take a break, a drink, a bite, and think it out. Next, send only one skier out on a likely line of travel with instructions to go only so far by his watch. This is the time to use whistles. Try to have plastic ones because they won't freeze to your lips in really cold weather.

If the searcher finds the trail or a position from which a number of landmarks are visible and your location can be pinpointed, he should whistle the party on, using an agreed code. If not, he should return and let another skier try another search spoke. Chances are almost nil that you will be lost or unsure of your exact location for very long. You can, of course, backtrack your trail by ski marks or blazes until you come to a known position.

Should worse come to worst, however, and you find that you really don't know where you are, that new snow has blanked out the back trail, and that night is coming on, make preparations to hunker down in safety. If your planning has been good, you will have with you what you need in the way of extra clothing, shelter, food, and fire. Come morning, you will be able to straighten things out. And in the unlikely event that daylight does not help you find the clues to your position, stay put and wait to be found. Don't let individual skiers go chasing off across the landscape convinced they know where home is. The safety of all lies in staying together.

At this point you will be very glad that you submitted an advisory on your plans for line and time of travel to the Forest Service, the Ski Patrol, and/or a good friend who will be concerned if you don't show up when you said you would and will sound an alarm. If you did not make such an advisory, mark yourself down as absolutely thoughtless and unsafe at ski touring.

But whatever your advisory situation, it's time to begin making a smoke signal and extending measured "spoke" trips seeking a recognizable landmark. Be careful. You have a problem; don't let concern make it worse. Maintain a fixed base; the mountain rescue teams are first-rate and will find you if you stay put near your signal. A final note on advisories: be sure that the Forest Service, the Ski Patrol, and your friend know that you are back from your trip, safe, sound, and happy. There is nothing worse than a wild goose chase in winter woods.

5 — Traveling to and in the High Country

If by some chance you were headed for Antarctica as a guest of a branch of the military, you could leave the worry to them. They are practiced in dealing with deep cold; you would be in competent, safe hands. They know the requirements of people and vehicles when the temperature is 40 or more degrees Fahrenheit below zero. Wind-chill factor is a constant in their daily routine on that frozen continent. They would be sure you were properly prepared for it.

But what if on your own you have decided to head into country that can and usually does experience Antarctic conditions once or twice a winter? Who has to be the cold weather expert? You. So if it is the Rocky Mountain High Country you are heading for, be prepared. It is reasonably certain that Antarctic conditions will grip that country for a brief blast a time or two each winter. I remember a 10-day period a few winters back when the best it could do was warm up in the daytime to 20 degrees Fahrenheit below zero. Everything just froze solid. Another winter, we stared in surprise one cold, still morning at the ice crystals hanging in the air. The thermometer read 57 below zero. Things just shattered in the cold. Not fit for man nor beast, that weather.

So welcome to the Rocky Mountain High Country. Yes, it can freeze up, and it is just good sense to be prepared for it. But remember, it is much more likely to be 10 or 20 degrees Fahrenheit above zero, the wind still, the sun out—just beautiful. Come along. But don't forget your long johns and flannel nighties.

By Airway and Railway

If you are flying or railroading to the High Country of Colorado, Utah, Arizona, or New Mexico from any significant distance away, you probably will be targeted to one of four main ports of call. These are Denver, Salt Lake City, Flagstaff, and Albuquerque. From these cities, lying at the feet of the Rocky Mountain ranges, you will go by car, bus, or smaller aircraft up into the snow country.

The major trunk airlines serving Denver are Braniff, Continental, TWA, United, and Western. Frontier Airlines provides service into Denver from a number of cities up and down the Rocky Mountains. Aspen Airways and Rocky Mountain Airways along with a number of smaller airlines and air services will carry you up to the small airports that serve the Colorado High Country ski resorts. The major carriers know the small airlines that serve the ski resort you are headed for and will make the necessary reservations at the same time you make your trunk airline travel plans.

Let's examine a few of the routings into Denver and the fares. We only will note the regular one-way coach fares. Be certain, however, to ask the airline reservations person whether they offer a "super-saver" or other special economy fare for the trip you are planning. There are any number of these special fares, and they seem to be changing all the time. Give special attention to the ski travel package fares that usually include ground travel and lodging costs. If the extra requirements of restricted travel periods and advance reservations and payment that accompany these fares don't trouble your logistics, the savings can be important.

Braniff provides a nonstop service into Denver from Dallas-Fort Worth for $79. You can also fly a one-stop to Denver on Braniff from Washington, D.C. Continental offers a number of daily flights into Denver from Los Angeles and Chicago. The fare from Los Angeles is $93 and from Chicago $99. TWA serves Denver from San Francisco but not from Los Angeles. The fare is $102. TWA also provides service from most of the major cities in the East.

There is no real fare competition among the airlines except occasionally in special fares (and when there is a difference, a quick game of catch-up is played) or when the routing between two points differs. TWA's Chicago-Denver fare is $99, the same as Continental's. (Fares do change now and then, so don't be surprised if you are quoted another figure than the one given here.)

United serves Denver from a number of points east and west. The fare from San Francisco is $102, from Los Angeles $93, from Chicago $99, and from New York $153. Western competes with United from Los Angeles and San Francisco at the same fares.

Salt Lake City is served by American through a number of flights originating at points in the East. The coach fare from Chicago to Salt Lake, for example, is $125. United will carry you to Salt Lake from San Francisco for $75, from Chicago for $125, and from New York for $179. Western offers service into Salt Lake from Los Angeles at $74 and from San Francisco at $75.

To get to Flagstaff you can fly American or TWA to Phoenix, where you will connect with Frontier. Albuquerque can be reached from the east and west by TWA. The Washington-Albuquerque fare, for example, is $154. From Los Angeles it is $80.

Air travel generally is a very good buy compared to other transportation forms, particularly when you count in its speed and frequency. But if speed is not your problem and trains are your passion, a trip by rail can be great fun. You are privileged to enjoy the scenery as well as healthy, change-of-pace relaxation.

Amtrak will be delighted to haul you from the east or west every day to all four mountain-city destinations. Denver and Salt Lake (through Ogden) are served from Oakland in the West and Chicago in the East. The one-way adult fare in coach from Chicago to Denver is $70. The Denver to Salt Lake stretch runs $39.50, and Salt Lake to Oakland is $62.

There is daily train service both ways to Albuquerque and Flagstaff; it is the same train. The run starts in the East at Chicago and in the West at Los Angeles. The one-way coach fare to Flagstaff is $35.50 from Los Angeles and $105 from Chicago. The costs for Albuquerque are $60 from Los Angeles and $88 from Chicago.

If you are planning to rent a car in any mountain doorstep city to drive on to your skiing destination, be sure to ask the auto rental firm to "skierize" the car for you. Most of them will at no extra charge, though you may be asked for a small deposit. The skierizing service generally includes a ski rack, an ice scraper and snow sweeper, and your option of snow tires, chains, or both.

Driving in the High Country

Should you plan to drive from your home base to the Rocky Mountains, you undoubtedly will take the above winter driving precautions and perhaps add a few more. First, be sure your battery is healthy and fully charged. Check the condition of your oil and consider changing to a lighter, winter grade if you do not already have it in. Your windshield washer fluid should be potent and able to withstand freezing temperatures. The level of protection of your anti-freeze should be checked. You want it effective well down below zero. And you might want to consider installing an electric engine heater that you can plug in on very cold nights. They make starting your car an easy pleasure on a freezing morning. If you do put one in, remember to bring along a heavy-duty extension cord just in case you can't park alongside the outdoor outlet that most mountain motels and camper parking areas now provide. A trouble light, road flares, and a shovel also are sensible precautions, as are an axe, a stout nylon line or tow chain, and heavy-duty jumper cables.

Major portions of the grid of interstate highways that cross or sweep along the lines of the mountain ranges in our four states are now completed. These roads are Interstate 15, 25, 40, 70, and 80. Of all of them, only I-70 in a stretch in Colorado from west of Vail to east of Grand Junction is a long way from completion.

Even these beautiful roads, however, can become difficult and even dangerous along with the older two-lane mountain roads when major winter blizzards attack. You not only will want to have taken all of the necessary precautions for yourself but also to be in a position to render assistance if that should become necessary. Along the well-patrolled interstates, professional help generally is available in a reasonable period of time for those in trouble. If you stop to help, make sure your vehicle does not compound the driving problems of others. On the two-lane roads, however, that crisscross through and over the mountains, help sometimes can be a long way off and a long time coming. The mountain ethic is to provide help if you can and to get help if you can't.

Driving on winter mountain roads covered with snow or spotted with icy stretches is not too difficult as long as your vehicle has been prepared for winter and you follow a few simple principles. Drive at a steady but slower than normal pace that lets you keep moving through the rough snow sections. The faster you drive, the faster you must maneuver the car to meet road conditions. And it is sudden maneuvers on snow or ice that usually trigger trouble. Try at all costs to avoid sudden steering or acceleration changes. Pump your brakes easily and steadily, don't jam them down and hold them. Easy does it all the time.

If you run into a series of drifts across the road, drive at a speed that lets you move through them easily, not explosively. Don't blast into them. Not only will it cut your visibility periodically, but when drifting snow is thrown up under the car it can jam the belts and even lift them right off the pulleys. You suddenly will have an overheated engine in the middle of a blizzard, with the pump no longer circulating coolant and a very difficult roadside repair job.

Should ice or wet snow accumulate on your windshield wiper blades, pull off the road in the first straight stretch you come to and clear them. Check for ice covering your headlights at the same time. It can build up enough to block them completely. In a heavy, blowing storm it is a good safety measure to have your lights on as a warning to other traffic.

In the event that you slip off the road into a bordering snowbank or slight ditch, try to keep the car moving steadily and steer at an easy angle back onto the road. If you stall, you still might be able to drive it out after a bit of work with the shovel. Remove the friction of the snowbank and dig an unblocked straight path back onto the road. Don't gun the engine; use steady pressure on the accelerator, and make sure that your front wheels are running reasonably true.

If there is a lot of muscle power in your group, maybe you can heave the car out. But don't break your back trying. People literally have cracked a vertebra in these situations. It is better to wait it out until help comes along. All that is required, generally, is a steady, straight tug from another car or pickup as you accelerate steadily. If the tug is from a four-wheel-drive vehicle, that's all to the good. Through all of these off-the-road operations, be sure that one of your party is stationed with a light so that he can warn oncoming traffic of your situation. And, of course, he can hail down help if that is needed.

Skid correction, of course, on snow or ice is just the same as on wet pavement. Turn the steering wheel in the direction of the skid. But the correction must be just enough to break the skid and let the power wheels grab and track again. If you overcorrect, too much and too jerkily, you might whip your car into a merry-go-round spin right off the road.

Should it appear that you are going to be stuck for any long period of time and the weather is cold and windy and likely to get worse, begin thinking about warmth and safety. There are far too many variables in these situations to set up hard and fast rules. Do what seems sensible, from going for help to setting up shelter. Remember, common sense is panic's enemy. Avoid sitting in the closed car for long periods with the engine running in order to operate the heater. Insidious carbon monoxide poisoning is always a threat in such situations. Another consideration is that a cold car sitting in the wind can just zap the heat from your body. Get out the extra clothing, the sleeping bags, or move to a better shelter situation, including a snow shelter if that can be done. If you leave the car, a rotating guard shift should be set up at the stranded vehicle to warn traffic and seek help. And if that can't be done because you don't have the clothing to meet the weather, be sure to leave a message in the unlocked car as to your whereabouts and need for help.

When parking your car or camper or other recreation vehicle in a specified parking area near a trail head, try to park so that you will not be snowed in by drifting snow. Also, if possible, park so that when you return you can drive straight ahead out of the area. If the starting run is downhill, so much the better. Do not set the parking brake unless you absolutely must; it might freeze. Leave the vehicle in "park" or a low gear.

Another sensible recommendation is to leave the keys hidden near the car or in a magnetic box attached to an out-of-sight part of the car body. If you should lose car keys while out cross-country skiing, you probably never will find them. Make sure that everyone in the party knows where the keys are just in case someone has to be sent forward to get help. And in your winterizing, be sure to dry-lube your car locks with graphite powder. That will help keep them from freezing and make them easier to open if they do. Heating the key while working it into the lock usually will solve the frozen-lock problem.

A smart safety precaution is to leave a note on the dashboard that is readable through the windshield. It should describe your travel plans, destination, and starting and estimated return times. If your car is still sitting there well after your estimated time of return, someone is sure to get word to the rangers or patrol, or they will spot it themselves during their rounds.

A camper or other recreation vehicle makes a fine base camp for short or long ski-touring trips. Be sure, however, that it is completely winterized so that things don't freeze up while you are out traveling in the snow.

Before parking on the plowed shoulder of a mountain highway it would be very wise to contact the local highway patrol office. Determine that they allow on-shoulder parking for the stretch of highway you have in mind. Should snow threaten while you are out touring, it probably would be well to cut your trip short and head back. Digging out a vehicle blocked by plowed snow is heavy work.

Using a car or other motor vehicle in the High Country to get to your cross-country trail should be and can be a safe and comfortable procedure. Just be sure you have taken all the proper precautions. If you have any doubts or questions, ask the locals. They are driving all winter long—as if it were nothing.

Traveling the High Country along the Continental Divide. *Sven Wiik*

Part 2

The Places

The Front Range of the Rocky Mountains is the first great barrier a traveler in the United States meets as he moves westward after crossing the worn and rolling Appalachians. The Rockies are rather like a set of huge mountainous rock waves, one behind the other. They rise up in various and sundry linked ranges running from the impressive to the merely rugged, as they move out of Canada, down the length of the United States, and on into Mexico.

But along their backbone they bear the Continental Divide. Here the massive watersheds of the eastern and western portions of the United States just touch before going their separate ways, with their creeks, streams, and rivers reaching for the Atlantic or the Pacific.

Farther to the west in a broken row run a number of parallel mountain ranges, many equally as wild and towering as the Rockies. The snow suitable for ski touring piles up on all of these heights that stretch from north to south across Colorado, Utah, New Mexico, and Arizona.

Only portions of these states, of course, offer the type of snow country that attracts Alpine and Nordic skiers from near and far. In Colorado it includes mostly the western half of the state. But near the border of Utah the land drops and flattens into broad sweeps of high desert, prairie, and canyon lands that run for some two hundred miles before the country rises again into the bold and skiable Wasatch Mountains. They overlook Salt Lake City and reach in a related string of ranges down through Cedar City into the southwest corner of Utah.

Over in New Mexico the snow-catching mountains are a large, blunt dagger of high country pointing down through the middle-top part of the state from Colorado, reaching almost to Albuquerque. Farther west in Arizona, skiing is pretty much restricted to the San Francisco Peaks around Flagstaff.

Most of the skiable snow land in these states is owned by the citizens of the United States. It is overseen by the U.S. Forest Service, the U.S. Park Service, or the Bureau of Land Management. But the facilities of lodging, food, and transportation are usually on private land. So on the following pages we will look at what is offered in the private ski resorts, the towns, and the national forests and parks that can support our ski-touring enthusiasm and allow us to give expression to it.

Rather than scout out and describe all of the nearly endless ski-touring trails and cross-country terrain of Colorado, Utah, New Mexico, and Arizona, we will seek to list the essential information that will let you decide where to head and whom to contact. Broad-brush descriptions of the terrain will give you some idea of what to expect when you move off on your cross-country skis. But a note to the wise. There is almost no stretch of country where, with but a little pre-planning, you cannot lay out a course that meets or challenges your competence. There is beginner, intermediate, and expert country just about everywhere. Do a little careful study of your topographical map, check it out with the Forest Service rangers or other local experts, and you will be off and ski touring, safe and comfortable or challenged and striving, just as you wish.

So come along, first to look at Colorado, then Utah, and, finally, New Mexico and Arizona, for the private and public ski touring areas: where they are, what they offer, and how you can reach them by phone and road.

6 — Colorado: Forests, Parks, and Private Ski Areas

When you are just considering the "lower-48," there is no question where the High Country is. It's Colorado. The average elevation is 6,800 feet. Of 67 mountains in the contiguous states with peaks above 14,000 feet, Colorado has 52. It is no wonder that skiers seeking the effervescence of High Country skiing in deep, dry snow have flocked to Colorado—Ski Country, USA.

And Colorado is not just for downhillers. Cross-country skiers find special treats there. Along the back of parts of the Continental Divide there are broad mountain meadows. In between the high ranges there are deep forests, rolling uplands, spur ridges and foothills, vast "parks" and high plateau farming country. All of this makes for a cross-country skier's paradise.

We talked earlier about how to get into the Rocky Mountain High Country. What we did not cover at that point was how to escape its mystique. There are no statistics, but it is a safe bet that more than half of the newcomers to Colorado in the past decade made their decision on a "first look" basis. And a very large number of them first came to Colorado as skiers. So beware of the siren snow of Colorado if you believe your roots are firmly anchored somewhere else.

National Forests and Parks

Much of the mountainous western half of Colorado is government land, with only the river bottoms and low foothills and the farm land along the western boundary in private hands. The private ski area operators own the land for their base operations, but they use their ski mountains under special use permits granted by the Forest Service. The surrounding mountainside and high country of most ski resorts is U.S. public land and the Forest Service encourages its multiple use by compatible, nondestructive interests. In wintertime the quiet ski tourer who leaves nothing but his tracks ranks first on their list.

There are 11 national forests in Colorado, and all of them to varying degrees may be used by cross-country skiers. Of all of them, the White River National Forest probably gets the heaviest usage. The reasons are its large size, the Interstate-70 corridor running through its middle, the great number of downhill ski resorts in the area, and its position in the snow-belt.

At the low end of this good-to-excellent scale are the forests on the eastern slope of the Front Range. The Pike and San Isabel along with the Roosevelt and a district of the Arapaho have problems when compared to western-slope forests. They suffer from variable snow conditions and wind. However, they still provide any number of good ski-touring opportunities, and the people of Denver, Colorado Springs, Pueblo, Boulder, Greeley, and Fort Collins put them to use.

To help you find out about snow conditions and ski-touring opportunities in the national forests of Colorado, we will list them all here. When you call, ask for the recreation officer. If he can't answer all your questions or if he thinks it might be more helpful, he might direct you to a particular forest ranger district on his or another forest. A number of the districts conduct well-organized ski-touring programs. We will look at five of them as a sampling.

Here are the national forest addresses and phone numbers. Some of the forests are under the same supervisor.

Arapaho-Roosevelt National Forests
Federal Building
3018 Howes Street
Fort Collins, Colorado 80521
(303) 482-5155

Grand Mesa-Uncompahgre National Forests
11th and Main Streets
Delta, Colorado 81416
(303) 874-7691

Gunnison National Forest (Shares the same address and telephone as the Grand Mesa/Uncompahgre National Forests but has its own supervisor.)
11th and Main Streets
Delta, Colorado 81416
(303) 874-7691

Pike-San Isabel National Forests
910 West Highway 50 West
Pueblo, Colorado 81008
(303) 544-5277

Rio Grande National Forest
1803 West Highway 160
Monte Vista, Colorado 81144
(303) 852-5941

Routt National Forest
137 10th Street
Steamboat Springs, Colorado 80477
(303) 879-1722

San Juan National Forest
701 Camino del Rio
Durango, Colorado 81301
(303) 247-4874

White River National Forest
Old Federal Building
Glenwood Springs, Colorado 81601
(303) 945-6582

To get a map showing the location of these forests of Colorado, or of another state discussed in this book, in terms of their relation to land features and developed areas, write to: United States Geological Survey, Building 41, Federal Center, Denver, Colorado 80225, and ask for the Colorado topographic map, scale 1:500,000. The price is $2.

Each national forest district is run by a team of forest rangers led by a district ranger. They institute and conduct programs in support of overall forest goals and also respond with special programs to meet the unique character of their district. When a district has the snow and terrain that make for good cross-country skiing, they strive within budget limitations to make it available in safety to ski tourers. So before touring off on any forest district, check in with the district ranger or his recreation officer. It only can add to your safety to have them know where you are going and when you are due back. And in all probability they will have a trail map of the area and some good advice.

There are far too many districts in the national forests of Colorado to note them all. But as a sample, we will take a look at the ski-touring support programs run by five of them.

Holy Cross Ranger District
White River National Forest
Box O
Minturn, Colorado 81645
(303) 827-5715

Winter snows run deep in the High Country of Rocky Mountain National Park, Colorado. *U.S. National Park Service*

Minturn is a few miles to the west and south of Vail. To reach it, drive past Vail on Interstate-70 to the U.S. 24 turnoff south of Minturn. The district ranger's office will have a packet of ski-touring information available that includes a number of cross-country safety guides and a selection of winter ski trail descriptions for their area. These single sheets have a marked map on one side and a complete description of the trail and pertinent information on the other. But it is easier to reproduce a sample ski-trail sheet than to describe it. Pictured is the Holy Cross District's Camp Hale Trail guide.

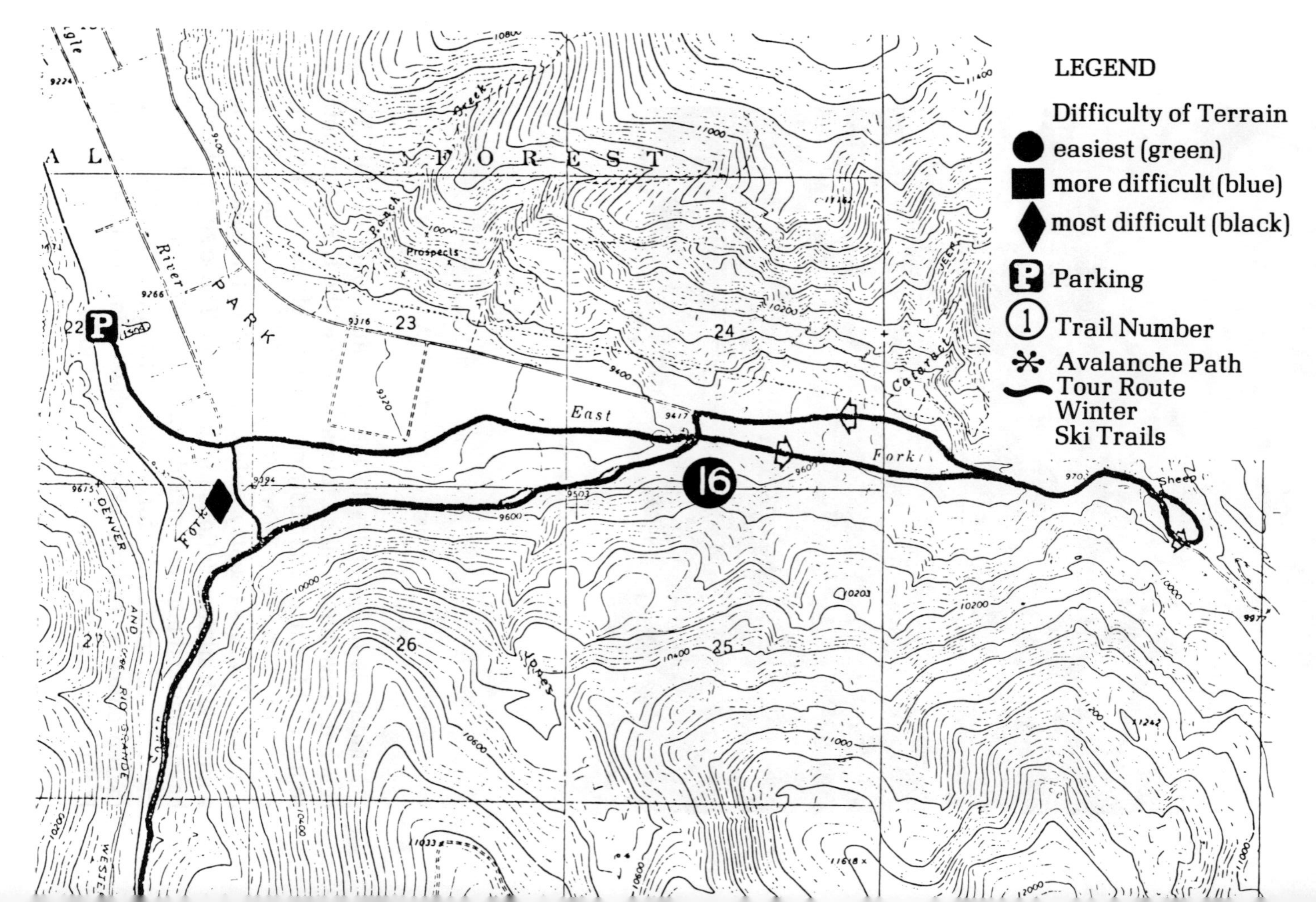

LEGEND
Difficulty of Terrain
easiest (green)
more difficult (blue)
most difficult (black)
Parking
Trail Number
Avalanche Path
Tour Route
Winter
Ski Trails
FOREST
PARK
River
East Fork
Prospect Canyon
DENVER AND RIO GRANDE WESTERN
23
24
25
26
27
16

CAMP HALE # 16
Holy Cross District, Miniturn, CO
White River National Forest
One day trip ŏr overnight
Distance: 9 miles (16.5 km) one way
Elevation gain: 566 feet (172.5 meters)
Maximum elevation: 9,832 feet (471.9 m)
Terrain: easiest
Topographic map: U.S.G.S. Pando, CO

The Camp Hale Trail is a network of one-way and two-way loops. Two-thirds of the trail is on flat terrain and provides all skiing abilities good trail to practice technique. The remaining one-third trail consists of three miles (4.8 km) of steady downhill or uphill skiing (depending on which direction you are travelling).

The road that continues from the east loop ends at the Climax Molybdenum Mine.

This area is not closed to snowmobilers however other areas are provided for the snowmobilers to discourage their use of this area.

Camp Hale used to be the training center for the famed 10th Mountain Division. In 1942, fourteen thousand U.S. Army men were trained here in mountain survival for combat during World War II. Skiing was one of the mountaineering skills acquired. Many of these same men were instrumental in the development of the ski industry in the United States today.

If you ski in areas not on the trail route and on the road beyond the east loop you will encounter avalanche terrain. For the weaker skier the South Fork Trailhead is recommended; the return will be downhill and flat.

A pond adjacent to the trailhead is the beginning for this trail. After skiing south across this pond and on the east side of two smaller ones, the trail will lead you across the south fork and parallel to the east fork of the Eagle River. Cross the Camp Hale Road and continue east eventually joining a spur of the Camp Hale Road. Ski along this road. The trail will turn to the southeast for a short stretch on the road then off the road north and finally west rejoining the road. This loop is a good spot to snack or lunch. The energy gained may be necessary later. When you resume, you will ski along the road to where it joins with another road. Turn southwest onto this road. You will climb gradually uphill, first in a westerly direction, eventually turning south until you reach U.S. Highway 24. The entire trip can be made shorter by cutting out various loops or simply turning back to the trailhead. For the advanced skier, the old "B Slope" used by the 10th Mountain Division, provides an exciting cross-country traverse down an open hillside.

The district office has maps for a total of five trails. But more are in preparation.

Leadville Ranger District
San Isabel National Forest
Box 970
Leadville, Colorado 80461
(303) 486-0749

The area around Leadville, because of its high elevation, is an exception to the more variable snow conditions and wind problems of the Front Range forests. You can pretty well count on this district in winter for good cross-country snow. But if you wish to check current conditions, call the district ranger.

At the Leadville district you will get a fold-up map that presents a collection of trails and loops with their descriptions. The map also has some general information on ski-trail classification, winter back-country ethics, the public use facilities program, and notes on trail markings and avalanche danger. But this composite map shows only some of the ski traills in the Leadville Ranger District. You can get information on other ski trails by contacting the district office.

Dillon Ranger District
Arapaho National Forest
Box 188
Dillon, Colorado 80435
(303) 468-2538

The Dillon district is a heavily used, all-season recreation area. The winter ski-touring trails generally are summer hiking trails. There is no winter maintenance on these trails, and only some of them are marked. If you take your 7.5-minute series map or an Arapaho National Forest visitor's map to the district ranger's office, you may copy over the information you want from the marked ski-trail map they keep there.

> Red Feather Ranger District
> Roosevelt National Forest
> 148 Remington Street
> Fort Collins, Colorado 80521
> (303) 482-3834

This eastern slope forest has some good ski-touring opportunities around Red Feather Lakes and Cameron Pass, which is at an elevation of 10,285 feet. The district office in Fort Collins will provide you with a map showing the ski trails in these two areas. Cameron Pass is 60 miles west of Fort Collins on state highway 14. Until the completion of an all-weather road in the summer of 1978, the end of the plowed road was the trail head. Now there is parking for ski tourers and a new patterns of trails around Cameron Pass.

> Taylor River District
> Gunnison National Forest
> 216 North Colorado
> Gunnison, Colorado 81230
> (303) 641-0471

To get to Gunnison from Denver, drive south on U.S. 285 for 135 miles to Poncha Springs. From there, it is a 60-mile run west on U.S. 50. The ranger district office has maps showing selected ski-touring routes around Ohio Pass (10,033 feet), in the Crested Butte area, and in the country surrounding the Taylor Park Reservoir.

Each skiable square mile of these districts and the countless thousands of other square miles of good cross-country ski terrain in the national forests of Colorado has its own charm and challenges. All the descriptions of rolling or steep, open or wooded terrain will provide you only with a very general guide to specific areas. Skiers will differ in their responses to trails and tours. The answer is to get out and discover for yourself which portions of the Rocky Mountain High Country appeal to you.

Two areas you might wish to add to your list of places to explore on cross-country skis are the U.S. Park Service's Rocky Mountain National Park and the Shadow Mountain Recreation Area, which abuts the park at its southwest corner. To travel to them by car from Denver, go west on Interstate-70 to the U.S. 40 turnoff at Empire, which will take you north to Granby. At Granby turn off onto U.S. 34 north to both the recreation area and the park.

Three linked lakes, Grand Lake, Shadow Mountain Lake, and Lake Granby (the last two are man-made reservoirs), make up most of the 29-square-miles of the recreation area, which is surrounded by the Arapaho National Forest and Rocky Mountain National Park. The Colorado River, whose sources are in the surrounding high country, is first named as it links Shadow Mountain Lake to Lake Granby. From Granby it starts its long run to the Gulf of California.

There are a few ski-touring trails in the area, mainly along the western edge of the lakes. But avoid touring on the lakes themselves. Thin ice near inlets and outlets is always a danger, and the water level under the ice of Lake Granby fluctuates.

Supplies and limited accommodations are available in the town of Grand Lake. Two miles north of town you can obtain information on the recreation area and the park from the visitor's center or by contacting the National Park Service, P.O. Box 100, Grand Lake, Colorado 80447, telephone (303) 627-3471. You can also get park and recreation area information from the Superintendent, Rocky Mountain National Park, Estes Park, Colorado 80517, telephone (303) 586-4425.

The Continental Divide marches down through the middle of Rocky Mountain National Park. The Trail Ridge Road (U.S. 34) linking Estes Park on the eastern slope to Granby on the western is closed during the winter. Access to the western side of the park with its extensive winter sport opportunities is limited to the U.S. 40 route to Granby and north on U.S. 34 through Grand Lake to the visitor's center. There you can learn current snow conditions as well as ski-trail information. The center will have a marked map and trail information folder that you can pack along with you. If you are planning an overnight trip, you will need a permit from the park ranger.

The road into the park is plowed for ten miles from the Grand Lake entrance. Eight trail heads are accessible from this road, four serving ski tourers and four serving snow-mobilers. Running off the "tunnel road" north of Grand Lake are three more trail heads. One of them serves both ski tourers and snowmobilers for a portion of its run. Though the map in the folder might suffice, it would be better to relate it to your 7.5-minute series topographical map and copy over the various trail markings.

Here is a typical trail description:

> D-GREEN MOUNTAIN TRAIL—Beginner to Advanced. Starting from the trail head 3 miles north of the Visitor Center offers the shortest route to Big Meadow (2 miles). Another trip possible from there is an all-day loop, by traveling up route C and down route D. The beginner, however, will find the best terrain in the valley floor. Park at the same trail head, but cross the road, ski past the cabins and into the meadow. Park land lies both to the north and south in this part of the valley.

A hike on touring skis up Homestake Creek, about 15 miles from Vail, Colorado. *Susan Biddle*

If ski mountaineering in Rocky Mountain National Park is of interest to you, ask the Superintendent to send you a tour guide prepared by the Rocky Mountain Nature Association. The brochure notes policies concerning winter travel in the park and provides brief information about terrain, equipment, weather, safety, avalanches, and suggested tours. There is no map in the brochure, so you definitely would have to plot out your route on a USGS topographic quadrangle. And that would be just the beginning of your preparations.

All the trips described in this brochure are on the eastern slope of the park, with the trail heads reached through the Beaver Meadows Entrance above Estes Park. Here is the description of one tour:

BEAR LAKE TO FERN LAKE AND MORAINE PEAK—a 10-mile trip for experienced ski mountaineers in excellent condition. All equipment should be pre-tested and parties attempting this one- or two-day tour should have equipment repair material, sufficient items for an emergency bivouac, and adequate clothing for severe wind and low temperatures. The first ½ mile of the route from Bear Lake is marked with red plastic arrowheads to the trail junction about halfway up the ridge north of the lake.

Turn left here and follow the trail to the top of the ridge, then west about ¼ mile. Use your topographic map and compass for the rest of the trip. Following the broad valley to the north and staying on the right side of the stream will lead you to Two Rivers Lake if you work your way to the left as you reach the upper part of the valley. The summer trail on the left side of the valley can be followed, but some of it is on a steep slope and snow cover is often poor in places. Follow this trail if you don't have a map and compass.

Cross Two Rivers Lake, after testing the ice, as usual, and ski the short distance west down to Lake Helene (check your map). To its right, the Odessa gorge appears. Descending, traverse down, staying out of any avalanche chutes. Looking up will verify this. Lacking skiing ability, take off skis or snowshoes and walk *straight down*, never getting in the avalanche chutes. After heavy snowfall, threatening masses of unsettled snow warrant aborting the trip down and turning back. Below, the right side of the valley leads naturally to Odessa Lake.

Beyond, follow the narrow gorge, staying to the right of the stream bed for ¼ mile. Cross the stream at a safe place, then follow it down on the left side, steering slightly away to the left as you do.

An overnight bivouac at Fern Lake is less windy than at Odessa. Below Fern Lake, the balance of the route follows the summer trail down to the Pool bridge. Beyond, the trail to Moraine Park is often dry in places; agile parties ski on the Thompson River ice to the trail head, where a second car has been left.

There is little need to stress the safety observations and precautions given in this description of a ski tour. By now you are aware that safety is the first standard by which to judge a cross-country trip.

When you know exactly where you are planning to ski tour, such trail descriptions can be of definite assistance. In the Appendix the detailed ski-trail guides that are available for portions of Colorado and other states in the Rockies are noted. Talking about your plans to rangers and other locals who ski tour also will be of great help in anticipating what you will meet on a particular trail. But your real knowledge will come as you travel it with a guide or with a map and compass. Observe that day's snow and weather conditions, and describe to yourself what they mean for ski tourers. Observe the relationship of major land forms and distinct landmarks. Observe, observe, observe.

Trail systems at the Devil's Thumb Cross-Country Ski Center in Fraser, Colorado, provide every type of challenge for the cross-country skier. *Sheldon Fingerman/Devil's Thumb Cross-Country Ski Center*

Since the above discussion deals with the eastern slope of the Rockies, it might be well to pause here and note that rapid and dangerous mountain weather changes are more likely there than on the western slope. But as the Nature Association's pamphlet goes on to note:

> Unpredictability is the key word for all mountain weather and is proverbial in the Rockies. The experienced Colorado mountaineer has shed all arrogance toward the weather and is prepared for extreme conditions.
>
> The Continental Divide, jutting into the prevailing west winds, is often capped by a turbulent and wet storm cloud.
>
> High winds, sometimes approaching 200 mph, are perhaps the greatest single weather danger in the [Rocky Mountain] Park. Above treeline, skiers may be blown off their feet and experience zero visibility, with a total loss of orientation. A skier enveloped in "white-out" may be moving downhill when he thinks he is standing still, or standing still when he thinks he is moving. The brittle, corrugated snow crust can snap ski tips unexpectedly. Skiers should stick closely together and retreat immediately to below treeline, cautiously probing for cornices, dropoff, etc.

Sounds scary, and it can be if you are caught in it. But if you have checked the weather in advance to make sure you are not climbing into a forecast storm, have pre-planned properly, are carrying the necessary equipment, and are touring with caution and forethought, you are not likely to get into serious trouble.

If you are planning anything longer than a day trip in the Colorado Rockies, you will need lodging. It can be either out in the snow or back at a base area. If a tent, snow shelter, motor home, trailer, or some other type of recreation vehicle is where you plan to bunk for the night, we will assume you have all the proper gear and know what you are about. In the towns around the parks and forests you will find motel or mountain inn lodging. The biggest supply of skier lodging, however, is in and around the base areas of downhill ski resorts. Since almost all of them now have cross-country programs, the rest of this chapter will list the major resorts and the cross-country centers that operate at them. There is no intent to the order in which these facilities are described other than a rough geographical grouping and relative size.

Privately Operated Ski Facilities

Vail
Ski Touring School
Box 819
Vail, Colorado 81657
(303) 476-5601, ext. 3268

There is a certain "richness" to Vail that cannot be denied, and it is of many orders. There is a richness of concept, a richness of skiable terrain, and a touch of richness to the people and prices. You can add to all of this other richness an excellent ski-touring school run by Steve Rieschl. While the prices

One can find immense recreational joys in the world of winter, as do these skiers traveling up Homestake Creek near Vail. *Susan Biddle*

may be a mite higher than elsewhere, as befits Vail, you get your money's worth in the quality of the school and of the cross-country terrain it uses for instruction and touring.

If it is your introduction to ski touring or to Vail, you probably will begin on the easy terrain of the golf course. Should you want to stretch your legs but stay in Vail, the golf course trail is part of a trail that runs from Park Meadows at the west end of town to Katsos Ranch in East Vail. For the more experienced there are runs along the nearby ridges and valleys. And the ski school offers 20 touring trips in and around Vail over trails picked for different skill levels. Most of these routes, which cover some 163 miles, glide through vistas of spectacular Rocky Mountain High Country in the White River National Forest.

Special forest service maps or ski-trail guide publications cover much of this country. If you are confident of your abilities and preparation, you might choose to go without a professional guide; however, a guide is recommended for most groups since trails are not marked or maintained and avalanche danger exists in certain areas. For more experienced skiers the school will arrange special powder excursions, combining adventurous touring with demanding technique. Many

Companions share their reactions as they head down to Red Cliff, Colorado.
Susan Biddle

of the trips for less experienced skiers start at Vail Pass and explore the surrounding terrain. A special treat is a nighttime tour, with skiers wearing miner's lamps and breaking the tour midway for a campfire feast.

All-day classes for $14 consist of a two-hour morning lesson and a two-hour afternoon tour. A half-day lesson or tour is $10. The cost of the all-day tour is $14. You bring your own lunch, but transportation to and from the trail head is provided. You may rent equipment through the ski school rental shop for $7 a day.

There are thousands of beds in and around Vail in a variety of accommodations. But in a typical winter season the demand is very heavy, and you will have to plan ahead. To get an idea of what is available and at what price, contact Vail Resort Associates, P.O. Box 1368, Vail, Colorado 81657, telephone (303) 476-1000. Vail, by the way, is 110 miles west of Denver on Interstate-70.

> Aspen Chamber of Commerce
> 328 East Hyman Avenue
> Aspen, Colorado 81611
> (303) 925-1940

The Chamber of Commerce also operates the Visitor Information Bureau. If yôu contact them about Aspen and ski touring, you will receive a small avalanche of literature.

Aspen Mountain Ski Corporation concentrates on downhill and leaves cross-country instruction, tour guiding, and rentals to a host of independent operators, most of whom have descriptive brochures that will reach you through the Chamber. Here are some of their names: Ashcroft Ski Touring Unlimited, (303) 925-1971; Aspen Mountaineering, (303) 925-1166; Fothergill's Outdoor Sportsman, (303) 925-3288; Mountain Guides and Outfitters, (303) 925-6680; Aspen Highlands Ski Touring, (303) 925-2464; Snowmass Ski Touring Center, (303) 923-4012; Boulder Mountaineer, (303) 925-2849.

You may deal with any of them for ski rentals, instruction, and tour guiding. If you want to head off on your own, however, there are any number of self-guided ski tours in and around Aspen. Here, in brief, are some of the most popular:

The Rio Grande Trail: Down the hill beyond the Jerome Hotel, going south on Mill Street, you come to the Rio Grande Trail as it crosses Roaring Fork River over a wooden footbridge. As you continue, there is a second footbridge where Hunter Creek enters the Roaring Fork. The old railroad bed continues down the valley, staying close to Roaring Fork River. You may take a short tour to the Slaughterhouse Bridge or continue on down the trail to Woody Creek.

Difficult Campground: Driving up Independence Pass (the top of the pass is closed in winter) about three miles from Aspen, you will come to the parking lot for Difficult Campground. You may ski into the campground, where there is a network of trails. This is a good trip for a cookout; there are grills in the campground.

Independence Pass: Continue driving up Independence Pass to the point where they stop plowing and where the road is barricaded. You may park there and ski tour on up to the pass. The elevation is 12,095 feet; the views east and west are spectacular.

Buttermilk-Snowmass: The start of the route is opposite the upper parking lot of Buttermilk West, where two yellow Forest Service signs mark the beginning of the trail. Most of the route is through Aspen trees and some evergreens. Many markings are by tree blazes and signs along the route to Snowmass.

Hunter Valley: This valley, located above Aspen, offers miles of gently rolling terrain that is enjoyable for tourers of all levels of ability. Park in the designated lot on Red Mountain.

Aspen Golf Course: The Aspen golf course has mildly rolling terrain that offers good practice and exercise. Drive west of Aspen to the Plum Tree Inn, where there is a parking lot. Several trails will be packed, or you may make your own.

Following are descriptions of a few of the cross-country specialists in Aspen.

Ashcroft Ski Touring Center, which offers all things to ski-touring men and women, needs to be examined in some detail because of its claim to fame as the first independent ski-touring area recognized by special use permit in the White River National Forest. It is located about 13 miles up the Castle Creek Valley from Aspen. Ashcroft is the site of an historic ghost town. You may drive there or take the courtesy bus, which leaves Rubey Park at the Mill Street Mall each morning at 9:15, arriving back each afternoon at approximately 4:30.

In the beautiful Alpine valley surrounding Ashcroft's King Cabin headquarters you will find 30 miles of mapped, marked, and maintained trails roaming the valley floor and scooting up the nearest foothills. The trails open at 8:30 and close at 4:00, seven days a week. The daily trail fee is $4, with children 8 years old and under admitted free. No skiers are admitted onto the track after 2:00 P.M.: you must check back out at King

Ashcroft Ski Touring Center, 13 miles up Castle Creek Valley from Aspen, Colorado. *Aspen Skiing Corporation*

Cabin. There are 3 warming huts along the trails, with potbellied stoves, and there is complimentary bouillon, hot chocolate, tea, and coffee. Daily rental for skis, boots, and poles is $7.

Guided off-trail day tours into the High Country can be arranged for minimum groups of four making reservations a day in advance. The cost is $16 a day per person, including lunch. Overnight tours to mountain cabins start at $25 per person for a picnic lunch, dinner, lodging, and breakfast plus two days on the trails. Back-country guided tours for parties of five or more can be arranged.

Mount Hayden looms in the background of the Ashcroft Ski Touring Center near Aspen, Colorado. *Aspen Skiing Corporation*

You may ski to your reserved lunch or dinner at The Pine Creek Cookhouse, 45 minutes up-trail from King Cabin. House specialties are Hungarian and Swiss dishes; there is a full complement of beer, wine, and spirits. Following the evening meal, guests are provided with miner's head lamps if there is no moon for the long glide down to King Cabin and the parking lot.

Chuck Fothergill's Outdoor Sportsman is one of the ski-touring mainstays in Aspen. Join a class at $8 a half-day or $12 for a day, or opt for a guided tour and you will be led off by Fothergill's certified instructors to glide wherever they think the snow is best. This might be on the packed trails in and around Aspen or up in the High Country on the fresh snow of some 200 miles of unmarked trails. Private lessons and private tours as well as overnight trips to back-country cabins can be arranged. Rental equipment runs $6 a day.

Mountain Guides and Outfitters ski school, staffed by experienced, professional mountain ski-touring guides, offers the usual platter of options. There is instruction for beginners, intermediates, and experts as well as guided day and overnight tours into the back country. Group lessons for beginners and intermediates are $8 a half-day and $13 for a full day, with full-day equipment rental running $6.50. Expert and advanced expert classes for the near-professional mountain skier are full-day lessons only. The cost is $13, plus a single lift ticket and $5 for lunch. Day trips into the back country start at $18.50 per person, with a mountain meal complete with appetizers and wine included. Overnight trips to heated mountain huts must be arranged in advance.

To drive to Aspen from Denver, follow Interstate-70/U.S. 6 west to Glenwood Springs. State highway 82 south leads to Aspen, which is 42 miles away.

> Steamboat Springs—Chamber & Resort Association
> P.O. Box L
> Steamboat Springs, Colorado 80477
> (303) 879-0740

Steamboat Springs really is two towns. In the late spring

summer, and fall it is the western ranch and farm town that came into being in 1875. But when the fields and pastures are lying quietly under deep winter snows, Steamboat becomes a bustling ski town, ranking right up there with Vail and Aspen. The town's ski history gives it a far better claim to "Ski Town-USA" than either of those two downhill meccas. In 1913 Carl Howelsen, the "Flying Norseman," arrived in Steamboat Springs with a new kind of "skeeing" and jumping Norwegian style. Cross-country skiing became and remains a very popular winter sport; ski jumping on Howelsen Hill is part of the life-style of the town's youngbloods; Alpine racing on Mt. Werner regularly attracts Olympic-level competitors.

The terrain around Steamboat is suited almost ideally for all levels of cross-country skiing. The Yampa River Valley is broad and rolling. Unplowed country roads and snow-filled fields abound. There is a ski-touring center on the golf course and other runs in Strawberry Park and on the Elk River. Trails climb up into the surrounding Routt National Forest. Along the Continental Divide near Rabbit Ears Pass there are miles and miles of rolling, partially wooded country for ski-touring adventure.

With all of this good terrain, naturally there are a number of

Ski tourers at Rabbit Ears Pass. Note the rock formation that gives the pass its name, and the unethical dog. *Sven Wiik*

operations devoted to ski touring. You may obtain brochure information on any or all of them by contacting the Steamboat Springs—Chamber & Resort Association.

Steamboat Ski Touring Center is a branch of the downhill base operator, LTV Recreation Corporation. Working out of the summer club house, the center runs some 20 kilometers of groomed and marked trails over the golf course. There is a trail fee of $1.50 a day. At the center you will find a restaurant and bar, a rental and retail shop for cross-country equipment, a warming area, and a professional cross-country ski school. Two-hour lessons, morning or afternoon, cost $9. If you want to tour away from the golf course, there is a half-day trip to Fish Creek Falls for $15 per person, with a minimum of four people required. An all-day tour to Rabbit Ears Pass or Hot Springs, again for a minimum four-person group, is $25 each and includes lunch.

Scandinavian Lodge is where "ski touring" is spoken almost exclusively. The lodge is among the leading, best-known cross-country centers in the United States. Sven and Birthe Wiik, the excellence of their program, the ski-touring terrain of Steamboat, and the charm of the lodge have most to do with its fame. It doesn't need much more. But Sven is a former U.S. Olympic ski coach; Birthe is a talented cook and a creative weaver and potter. The lodge is tucked off in the woods on a high shoulder of Mt. Werner. It is warm and personal, an old-fashioned "family" lodge. The ski-touring terrain of Steamboat already has been described; the lodge offers 20 miles of free, marked, and maintained trails as its contribution to the total.

Long before the current popularity of cross-country skiing, Sven Wiik was carrying the message by laying out trails and conducting clinics. Today, that educational effort is continued season-long at the Scandinavian Lodge, with clinics for the National Ski Patrol, ski-touring business people, cross-country racing coaches, and national conservation groups.

A full-day rental of equipment is $6. A half-day group lesson is $5.50 per person. For an hour and a half private lesson the charge is $11 per person, with no more than two people per instructor. Guided ski tours are $5.50 per person for a half day, $9 per person for a full day.

When you put up at the Scandinavian Lodge, you will have the pleasures of three full meals a day under the American Plan. If you take lodging in the condominium apartments, you are on the European Plan. Other facilities available to all guests at the lodge are a sun room and swimming pool, four saunas, a gymnasium, and quiet reading rooms.

Glen Eden Ranch is to be found by going north from Steamboat Springs up the Elk River toward Steamboat and Pearl Lakes and the Mt. Zirkel Wilderness Area. This run takes you through some of the finest ski-touring terrain in the Steamboat area. Glen Eden Ranch is 18 miles north of Steamboat in the Elk River Valley; all around is the rising High Country of the Routt National Forest.

The Glen Eden is a traditional Western guest ranch, but in the winter season its ten-gallon is tipped to cross-country skiers. The comfortable, warm lodge, with its restaurant and Fireside Lounge, is in the midst of a cluster of mountain cabins that offer complete housekeeping facilities.

The 14 miles of private cross-country trails maintained by the ranch are graded for beginners, intermediate, and experienced cross-country skiers. All the trails begin at the lodge; there is no trail fee. Guides, special tours, and overnights can be arranged by advance reservation. Equipment rental is $5 a day.

Vista Verde Guest Ranch is a place for ski tourers to "get away from it all" in a more than usual cross-country fashion. Frank Brophy's Vista Verde is a working, 600-acre cattle ranch. It is 25 miles northeast of Steamboat Springs on Seedhouse Road, which runs to the east off Elk River Road (state route 129) just past Clark.

Located near the main lodge, with its large fireplace and recreation area, are six hand-hewn log cabins with kitchens and fireplaces. Wintertime rates for one or two people are $30 per night, three people for $40, and each additional person $5 to a maximum of six people.

These rates include the use of 10 miles of groomed trails on the ranch and access to marked trails in the surrounding Routt

National Forest. Guided group tours onto the Routt for half-day ($5) and full-day ($9) are available, as is an overnight tour to a log cabin at the base of the Mt. Zirkel Wilderness Area.

Group lessons cost $4 per person for an hour and a half; private lessons run $8 for an hour and a half. Meals are not served in the lodge during the winter months; special lunches and dinners can be arranged in advance.

Bear Pole Ranch is a ski lodge in the winter season and the home of Discovery, Expedition and Adventure Bound groups of young people in the summer months. This rustic ranch, a few miles north of Steamboat Springs in Strawberry Park, offers cross-country skiers a selection of rolling meadows, low forest-ed ridges, and deep back country on the nearby Routt National Forest. If the skier's interest should shift to downhill for a day or two, Steamboat's Mt. Werner is only 15 minutes away by special ranch buses.

One way to look at the surrounding High Country is to take your touring skis up the long, winding unplowed road leading to Buffalo Pass. As you climb you will have increasingly im-pressive views of the Yampa Valley and the surrounding mountain ranges. The run back down will be well worth the climb.

A one-hour lesson is $3. Rentals are $5 a day or $4 a day for three days or more. A half-day guided tour is $4, and a full day runs $7, with $2 extra for lunch. Special moonlight tours and tours to the hot mineral springs are available.

Big, wholesome meals are served buffet style, and there is evening recreation in the "baen." For information on special tour packages with accommodations in fireplace-warmed cabins or dormitory units, contact Dr. and Mrs. Glenn Poulter at Bear Pole Ranch, Star Route 1, Steamboat Springs, Colorado 80477.

Mountaincraft, located on the main street in the heart of this small Western town, offers a complete service to the cross-country skier and ski mountaineer. There is new equipment for sale and quality equipment for rent. Maps and compasses, cooking gear and freeze-dried foods, tents and sleeping bags, and just about anything else a mountain person might need is on display. The staff is experienced and prepared to discuss the merits of different pieces of gear. Instruction can be arranged, along with guided tours through the High Country around Rabbit Ears Pass. And if you just want to talk touring, the Mountaincraft people do that without charge.

Equipment rents for $3 a half-day and $5 for a full day. A full-day lesson and tour costs $8 per person for a group of three or more and $10 per person for two. Half-day rates run $5 per person for a group of three or more and $6 per person for two.

> Breckenridge
> Ski Touring School & Mountain Guide Service
> P.O. Box 1058
> Breckenridge, Colorado 80424
> (303) 453-2368

As an encouragement to its beginning students, the touring school emphasizes the leisurely aspect of cross-country skiing with a French phrase: "Balade dans la neige" (A stroll in the snow). To take them from that beginning to ski touring in the High Country of Summit County, the school is organized into four class levels, with instruction by certified professionals. Class A includes introduction to equipment, waxing, and beginning techniques on level terrain and gentle slopes. The cost is $7. The class and a short afternoon tour, combined, is $10. Class B ventures out on short afternoon tours on gentle trails, giving students a chance to perfect their new skills. The cost is $7. All-day tours in the Ten Mile Range and along the Continental Divide with visits to some of the old prospecting areas are the stuff of Class C. The charge is $10 and you bring your own lunch. The school has more than 5 miles of trails for novices, 15 miles for intermediates, and near-endless untracked mountain country for advanced skiers. Class D is designed to make the intermediate skier an advanced ski tourer. Two-hour classes cost $7. Instruction is given in the fundamentals of the stem christie, stem turn, parallel turn, telemark turn, and powder skiing.

The Mountain Guide Service will take minimum groups of four at $20 a person on overnight tours on High Country trails and through back-country powder. Moonlight ski tours with a break for hot wine and cheese fondue also are available with advance reservations. The complete price is $15 per person for a minimum group of four.

Equipment rentals, running between $5 and $6.50 a day, are available at many of the area ski shops. You also will be able to pick up a cross-country trail map for the area in the shops.

To reach Breckenridge take Interstate-70 west from Denver through Dillon to state route 9 south. Breckenridge is 9 miles south of the turnoff.

Copper Mountain
Ski Escape/Ski Touring School
Box 1
Copper Mountain, Colorado 80443
(303) 668-2882

A free 35-kilometer system of marked and maintained trails covering a variety of terrain branches out from the ski-touring center at Copper Mountain. Those trails plus High Country trails and touring terrain in the surrounding Gore Wilderness Area and Ten Mile Range place this center in the middle of some of the finest mountain ski touring to be found anywhere.

An introductory morning class is offered daily for $7. A full-day session, which combines an afternoon tour with morning instruction, is $9. More advanced classes can be arranged on an advance reservation basis; the charge is $9.

In addition to day tours, overnight tours, and moonlight tours, the Copper Ski Escape Center on Thursday evenings conducts a guided tour to an old mountain cabin where a gourmet-quality, old-American family-style dinner is served. Kerosene lamps, a wood burning stove, and an introduction to the history of Summit County take the diners back to the time of the early settlers.

Equipment rentals at the center are $6 for adults and $4 for children per day. A lift ticket exchange program encourages the downhill skier to explore cross-country. The daily lift ticket entitles the skier to a $5 lesson starting at 2 P.M., with equipment included. That should get some of the downhillers off the pack and into the woods.

Copper Mountain is one and three-quarters hours west of Denver on Interstate-70.

Keystone
Bo 38
Keystone, Colorado 80435
(303) 468-2316, ext. 3868

Six and one-half miles of marked and maintained trails in and around Keystone Village and along the banks of the Snake River are combined with 20 miles of marked trails that climb out of the village to provide something for every level of ski-touring skill. Off-trail skiing will lead you past old mining ghost towns and to tremendous High-Country views of the Continental Divide. Keystone is located in the Arapaho National Forest.

The First Gear Sport Shop is the center for ski touring at Keystone. Group lessons are $7 for a single session of an hour and a half and $12 for a double session. Picnic lunch tours are $12, with lunch included. Guide service into the back country is available. Equipment can be rented at First Gear for $6 a day.

Lodging is available in the Keystone Lodge and in a number of condominium units at the base of the mountain. Other lodging is available in Dillon, five miles down the road.

Keystone is 72 miles west of Denver via Interstate-70 to Dillon. At Exit 39 take U.S. 6 east for five miles to Keystone.

Tour the Summit
Breckenridge, Copper Mountain, Keystone

The miles of ski trails and cross-country terrain of Summit County now are available to ski tourers through a unique program that links the trail systems of Breckenridge, Copper Mountain, and Keystone. Join the program at any of the three ski-touring schools. You will be taken to a neighboring area and greeted by a Nordic instructor who will take you on an all-day tour with a wine and cheese picnic lunch. The fee is $12. Plans are underway to link these three areas with a trail/hut system, similar to European systems, that will open up a vast expanse of touring terrain to the experienced skier.

For details on this program, contact the ski-touring schools at any of the three ski resorts. Their addresses and phone numbers are given with their listings.

Idlewild
Ski Touring
Box 3
Winter Park, Colorado 80482

Just a ski-pole throw from well-known Winter Park is a small Alpine and Nordic ski resort called Idlewild. It combines a good Alpine beginner's program with a highly developed ski-touring program that has over 30 kilometers of marked and maintained trails. A beginner's trail wanders along the Fraser River. Intermediate trails explore rolling and more difficult terrain as they climb into the surrounding Arapaho National Forest. Advanced ski-touring trails are reached from the top of the Alpine lift.

Rentals run $6 a day. Full-day class lessons are $9 and half-day $6. An all-day lunch tour with instruction costs $12. The red barn at the base is the ski-touring center. It has a retail shop in addition to the rental shop. Arrangements can be made here for guided photography tours and overnight guided trips into the Arapaho.

The Idlewild Lodge offers modified American Plan lodging. Among its facilities are a heated outdoor pool, steam bath, game rooms, and a cocktail lounge.

You reach Idlewild from Denver by traveling west on Interstate-70 to the Empire turnoff. Take U.S. 40 west over the Berthoud Pass. Idlewild is just beyond Winter Park.

Devil's Thumb Ranch
Cross Country Center
Box 125
Fraser, Colorado 80442
(303) 726-8298 and 726-8155

Getting off to a good start at Devil's Thumb Ranch and Cross-Country Ski Center in Fraser, Colorado. *Sheldon Fingerman/Devil's Thumb Cross-Country Ski Center*

This old-established ranch with rustic lodge and cabins— the official Rocky Mountain Training Site for the U.S. Cross-Country Ski Team—is set in a broad, gently rolling valley with 50 kilometers of marked trails bordering on the Arapaho National Forest. To the east of the ranch are the towering, snow-covered mountains of the Continental Divide.

The ski-touring program at Devil's Thumb is directed by Dick Taylor, former U.S. Olympic Team captain and present regional coach for the U.S. Cross-Country Team. Taylor personally designed the trail system to provide every type of cross-country challenge. The maze of touring tracks and alternate routes is roughly divided into one-third climbing, one-third fast downhills, and one-third rolling and flat terrain. You may seek out a track, all of which are maintained, to meet any level of skill. For the racer there is a 15-kilometer International Class track designed to F.I.S. standards.

The courses are open each day from 9 A.M. to 4 P.M., with a $2 a day track fee. One and a half hours of group instruction runs $6; private lessons are $12 for one and a half hours, and racing instructions is $15 for the same time period. That fee

Rustic lodge at the Devil's Thumb Cross-Country Ski Center, Fraser, Colorado. *Sheldon Fingerman/Devil's Thumb Cross-Country Ski Center*

includes a video tape of your performance. With three days notice the center will arrange all-day back-country tours that include discussions on technique, supplies, and safety precautions. The cost is $13 and includes a packed lunch. Rental equipment runs $6 a day and $4 a half-day.

To reach Devil's Thumb take Interstate-70 west from Denver to U.S. 40 west at the Empire turnoff. Fraser is west of Winter Park. Look for Cabin Creek Road and Devil's Thumb Ranch about three miles west of Fraser.

There are cabins and lodge rooms available for families, couples, and groups. Hearty meals on the modified American Plan are served in the main lodge dining room that looks out across Ranch Creek Valley meadows to the peaks of the Divide.

Crested Butte
Ski Touring Center
Box 528
Crested Butte, Colorado 81224
(303) 349-6611

A stop for refreshments at the Cross-Country Ski Center, Fraser, Colorado. Hearty meals on the American plan also are available. *Sidney Fingerman/Devil's Thumb Cross-Country Ski Center*

Crested Butte, about 25 miles south of Aspen as the crow flies but a long way around by road, is tucked deep in the surrounding Gunnison National Forest. Much of the terrain in the area is ideal for cross-country skiing, and the Crested Butte ski-touring center is taking full advantage of it. The 19 kilometers of marked and maintained trails overlook the East River Valley, traversing rolling terrain, flats, and downhill powder runs. A 6-kilometer race-course track forms part of these trails. More than 160 kilometers of nonmaintained trails, which are jeep roads in the summer, range through and over the valleys and ridges near the Alpine area.

Rates for lessons are $8 for a two-and-a-half-hour morning session. A half-day tour is $8 and a full-day tour $12. If you combine a half-day lesson and a half-day tour, the price is $12. A packaged lunch for the day tour is optional at $4. One-day rental for a full set is $6, with gaiters provided free by the Whetstone Ski Rental Shop. The Whetstone also is the place to sign up for tours.

Crested Butte is located 30 miles north of Gunnison on state route 135. Total number of driving miles from Denver is 228.

Peaceful Valley
Ski Touring Center
Star Route
Lyons, Colorado 80540
(303) 747-2582

This eastern slope ski-touring center, only 45 minutes from Boulder on state route 72, is unique in having the only snow-making facility exclusively for Nordic skiing. The snow-making gun is insurance against the variable snow conditions of the eastern slope and guarantees good snow conditions for lessons in an area north of the lodge. Certified instructors use the area for training classes in both flat track and slope skiing. In addition to instruction, guided tours through the Front Range start from the lodge and visit very scenic areas, with views of the sweeping grasslands to the east and the jumble of the Rockies to the west.

Group rates are $5.50 for a half-day and $10 for a full day. Tour rates are the same. Equipment may be rented at the lodge for $5 a day or at sport shops in the metropolitan area below. The standard three-day, double-occupancy per person rate at Peaceful Valley Lodge is $103. This includes nine meals and two lessons or tours.

To drive to Peaceful Valley from Boulder, take state route 119 west to Nederland. Turn north on state route 72. Peaceful Valley Lodge is four miles before the junction of state routes 72 and 7.

Lake Eldora
Ski Touring Program
P.O. Box 430
Nederland, Colorado 80466
(303) 447-8012

The 22 kilometers of marked and maintained touring trails running through the wildlife sanctuary surrounding Lake Eldora are restricted to the wildlife and ski tourers in the winter. That means no dogs and snowmobiles. The trail fee is $2 for an adult, $1 for a child, and free for those 65 and over. For racing and training sessions, there is a 5-kilometer maintained track.

A two-hour group lesson is $7.50 and a full-day lesson is $11. This includes the trail fee. Rentals from the ski shop are $7 a day. Certified instructors, in addition to giving lessons, also will guide advanced skiers on tours into high country of the surrounding Roosevelt National Forest.

Food and drink are available at the Lake Eldora base lodge, which is five miles west of Nederland off state road 119. Lodging is available in Boulder, which is about 20 miles east of Nederland.

Beaver Village Touring Center
Box 43Q
Winter Park, Colorado 80482
(303) 726-5741

Three different day tours are offered each week by the Nokhu Mountain Guides. The Elk and Eagles Nest tour is offered twice a week. The guides skirt their groups past elk on their winter range and point out the nests of bald eagles. The cost for the all-day trip is $14 and includes transportation and lunch. On the Alpine Skinny Sticking tour the group climbs above the tree line to a hut for lunch. In the afternoon they ski snowbowls near Berthoud Pass. The fee is $14 and again includes transportation and lunch. And for those who like to take a warm and restful break during a ski tour, the touring center offers the $18 Colorado Hot Springs ski tour. Take along a towel.

A half-day lesson is $5 and a full-day lesson, $9.50. Rental equipment is $6 the first day and $4 for each additional day.

A 55-kilometer system of marked trails starts near the Beaver Ski Chalet. Only a few segments of the system require advanced cross-country skills. The trails are ski-packed, not groomed.

The touring center is in the Beaver Ski Chalet, which is near the Winter Park base area. Take U.S. 40 north from Interstate 70.

Colorado Outward Bound School
945 Pennsylvania Street
Denver, Colorado 80203
(303) 837-0880

Operating out of their new Mountain Center, which is just outside Leadville, Outward Bound conducts a variety of intensive ski-mountaineering and ski-touring courses in the rugged high country of the Collegiate Range. Two 21-day-long courses in ski mountaineering are offered each winter. Classes are formed into patrols of eight to ten skiers who have comparable skiing abilities. Each patrol is accompanied by an instructor and an assistant instructor. Equipment is a short downhill ski with a Slivretta-2 binding that will take a mountaineering boot. Patrol members shoulder heavy packs containing all the equipment they will need during their snow cross-country trip. The 21-day course is the same as Outward Bound's summer sessions except that the travel is on skis. There is a training period, a mountain expedition, a three-day solo trip, and a race. The $625 price is all-inclusive.

A number of 10-day short courses are offered during the winter. One, using Nordic gear for extended touring, is $325. Another, emphasizing ski mountaineering and avalanche training and using the same equipment as the long course, is $375. A Nordic course for men over 30 years of age costs $400.

San Juan Alpine Tours
Box 457
Silverton, Colorado 81433
(303) 387-5423

Situated in the picturesque old mining town of Silverton and surrounded by some of the most beautiful mountain country in Colorado, San Juan Alpine Tours offers a variety of extended ski-touring trips throughout the winter. The 15-day ski-mountaineering courses commence with a few days of instruction and touring before setting off for the selected area. The cost is $350, which includes lodging at the Teller House Pension and food at the French Bakery Restaurant. Equipment rental is $25.

Five-day courses are given for beginner and intermediate ski tourers. There also are five-day courses in ski mountaineering for more advanced skiers. The fee for these courses is $125. Rental equipment is $15 extra. Full- and half-day instruction, as well as daily equipment rental, also is available.

Silverton is on Colorado state route 789, approximately midway between Durango and Montrose. There is air service to both these cities.

> Rocky Mountain Expeditions
> Box CC
> Buena Vista, Colorado 81211
> (303) 395-8466

Using the San Isabel and Gunnison national forests are their touring grounds, Rocky Mountain Expeditions offers customized ski tours for groups of two or more. The price per person, naturally, varies with the size of the group.

For a touring party of two the price is $200 per person for two days, $340 for five days, and $400 for seven days. If there are six in the group, the per-person price for two days drops to $125, for five days it is $200, and for seven days $250. These prices include the guide fee, food, and camping equipment. Depending upon the wishes of the group, the evening meal and overnight rest will be in a heated mountain cabin or a tent camp.

The trips usually include cross-country technique instruction, survival skills, and an emphasis on the wilderness philosophy of "Leave nothing but your tracks." Equipment rental is $5 per day, $9 for a weekend, and $25 for seven days.

Rocky Mountain Expeditions is headquartered on the north side of town on U.S. 24. Buena Vista is 94 miles west of Colorado Springs.

Telluride Ski Touring
Box 672
Ophir, Colorado 81426
(303) 728-4316

There was gold in them thar hills. Now they are full of white powder. And with Telluride Ski Touring you can slide off into that deep snow and explore the once booming but now deserted mining towns in the high country around Telluride. There are miles and miles of ski-touring terrain around Telluride, but only those trails near the downhill ski area are marked and maintained. No trail fee is imposed.

A three-day beginner's program for groups of three to five people costs $26 per person. The first day is divided into a morning of instruction and an afternoon of practicing on the trail. The second day is spent in the quiet, snowbound stillness of the back country. The third day is another trip into the back country and an introduction to basic ski-mountaineering skills.

Other options are a starlight tour with wine, followed by a swim and sauna and then dinner. The price is $15. Overnight tours are made to a stone and wood chalet—complete with sauna and Jacuzzi—on Alta Lakes. Dinner and breakfast are included in the $35 per-person group price.

Equipment may be rented at either the Telluride Sports or Olympic Sports shops. The prices start at $4.50 per day.

Telluride is on state road 145. Commercial aviation can carry you to Durango, Montrose, or Grand Junction, all of which are within reasonable driving range.

7 — Utah: Forests, Parks, and Private Ski Areas

When Brigham Young, the early Mormon leader, arrived in the Salt Lake valley in 1847, he took one look around and pronounced: "This is the place."

That same judgment has been made any number of times more recently by swarms of skiers arriving in Salt Lake City for the first time and looking up at the snow-covered Wasatch Mountains. It's a thought hard to suppress when you realize that standing mid-city you are only minutes from some of the greatest powder skiing in the world. Downhillers thrill to the promises of Alta, Snowbird, Park City, and other famous Utah ski resorts. And well they should. The mountains are high and steep, the snow is deep and powdery, the season is long, and the sun is bright.

Many of these same snowy marvels work a powerful attraction on cross-country skiers as well. But for much of Utah's mountain country, the level of skill and knowledge necessary to ski tour in safety goes well beyond that needed for meadowland ski touring or loop-track running. Ski touring in much of the Wasatch demands that you know the country,

96

for the trails generally are not marked; that you understand and know how to avoid avalanche danger, for it is very real; and that you sensibly plan ahead for emergencies because, as the Forest Service notes, "winter is an unforgiving season."

A number of the downhill ski areas have a passive policy of not encouraging cross-country skiers. Some part of this feeling might stem from the difference in financial return between downhillers and ski tourers. But the far more important reason is the hazard that untrained or unprepared cross-country skiers can bring to themselves as well as to search and rescue parties.

In the vicinity of the more northern ski areas of Utah there are great stretches of snow-covered land suitable for ski touring. The number of marked trails, however, is few. When out on a day or half-day tour, it is easy to be charmed by the country into voyaging off across the ridges without particular plan. Unless you know the country well or are with a qualified guide, you might get into trouble.

One special hazard is "white out." This occurs when clouds bump into mountains. It can happen here when low clouds cross over the Great Basin and Great Salt Lake to the west. Their moisture is often water droplets, but as these clouds are forced up over the high, winter mountains, their moisture is more likely to be ice crystals. Either way, you have a fog, which is just the term for a cloud touching the ground. The sunlight filtering down through the fog—and there can be enough sunlight even on cloudy days—reflects off the snow and turns the fog's ice crystals as white as snow. You are in a "white out"; suddenly you have no references for distance, direction, or size. Up can look like down. A cliff might appear to be level ground. And your companions might disappear in just a few feet. You are surrounded by a close world of "snow."

The best response to the situation is to stay put. Clouds move on. If you must move, do it by compass headings of which you are sure. Stay together. Should you go blundering about, the threat of injury is real and your chances of becoming the object of a search-and-rescue mission climb.

Don't let these warning words keep you away from Utah, however. There is a plentitude of great cross-country skiing areas, there are marked and maintained trails, and there are qualified touring and ski-mountaineering guides.

National Forests and Parks

The national forests that have the mountains of principal interest to ski tourers are the Wasatch-Cache (two separate forests under one supervisor) and the Dixie. The Wasatch-Cache forests are in the northern part of the state and are marked on their western edge by Interstate-15 and the cities of Salt Lake, Ogden, and Brigham, One part of the Wasatch extends off to the east and shares the Uinta mountain range with the Ashley National Forest. The Uinta Mountains have

Skiing the High Uintas in Utah. *Pat McDowell*

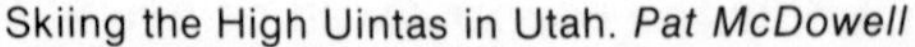

two interesting distinctions: they boast the highest point in Utah, Kings Peak at 13,512 feet, and they are the only important range in the United States to run east and west.

The Wasatch Range, running roughly north and south, forms the backbone of the state. It divides the drainage of the Colorado River from that of the Great Basin, once a great inland sea that was subsequently named Lake Bonneville. The Dixie National Forest covers the southern end of this range. Again, Interstate-15 runs along the forest's western edge; Cedar City is the major community. There are a number of private ski operations in this end of the state. And blocked out of the Dixie are two National Park Service areas that have particular interest for ski tourers: Cedar Breaks National Monument and Bryce Canyon National Park.

Here are the government forest and park addresses and phone numbers from which to get general and snow information for their areas:

Wasatch-Cache National Forests
8226 Federal Building
125 South State Street
Salt Lake City, Utah 84138
(801) 524-5030

Dixie National Forest
82 North 100 East
Cedar City, Utah 84720
(801) 586-2461

If you know where you are planning to head in the Wasatch-Cache National Forests, you might want to call the ranger district that has responsibility for the area. Ask for the information manager. The district that includes the ski operations at Alta, Brighton, and Park City is the Salt Lake Ranger District. That phone number is (801) 524-5042. Farther north is the Ogden Ranger District, which has a number of ski resorts and much cross-country terrain in its area. The number for the district is (801) 399-6431. And still farther north is the Logan Ranger District on the Cache. The recreation ranger for that district can be reached at (801) 752-1593.

In the Dixie National Forest much of the skiable terrain is on the Cedar City Ranger District. The number there is (801) 586-4462. It is a five-hour run down I-15 from Salt Lake City to Cedar City. Both Cedar Breaks National Monument and Bryce Canyon National Park are reasonably near to Cedar City. We will explore in some detail those two National Park Service areas and Utah's Wasatch Mountain State Park before reviewing the cross-country facilities available at private ski areas in Utah.

Cedar Breaks National Monument
82 North 100 East
Cedar City, Utah 84720
(801) 586-9451

Cedar Breaks is a 10-square-mile multicolored ampitheater slowly being eroded out of the western edge of Utah's High Country. Early settlers used the term "breaks" for badlands and misidentified the junipers growing near the base of the cliffs as "cedar." Hence the name. (You can pick up an informative map at the Superintendent's office in Cedar City.) To get to Cedar Breaks, drive east from Cedar City on state road 14 for 23 miles. Then it's just 3 miles north to the monument. It would be well to check road conditions before leaving Cedar City.

Park at the visitor's center, which is closed in winter, and go sliding on your touring skis out along the winding, five-mile Rim Drive. You will have sweeping views of the breaks and the surrounding High Country of the Dixie National Forest. On Rim Drive, the elevation is in excess of 10,000 feet. Take it easy if you are just up from the lowlands.

The surrounding Dixie National Forest has some fine terrain for ski touring. However, there are no marked and maintained trails. A few miles up the generally unplowed road toward Parowan is the Brian Head ski resort. A tour up this road will lead you to the creature comforts of the base area.

If you plan to stay overnight, lodging can be found in Cedar City and Parowan as well as at Brian Head.

Bryce Canyon National Park
Bryce Canyon, Utah 84717
(801) 834-5322

The last 15 miles of the Bryce Canyon Park rim road are not plowed in the winter. This trek, along with a number of other marked trails, makes for a ski-touring facility fit for the skills of all levels of skiers. Pick up a map at the visitor's center after entering the park; the ranger will give you assistance with it. You also will be asked to check in and out, but there is no charge for the use of the park. If you plan on an overnight, you will need a permit.

Winter lasts from November through March, but the days often are crisp and sunny. A call ahead to learn conditions, however, is probably worth it. Bryce is reached from U.S. 89 (which runs parallel to and east of I-15) from Bryce Junction, seven miles south of Panguitch and about the same distance north of Hatch. Lodging can be found outside the park or back in Cedar City.

Wasatch Mountain State Park
P.O. Box 218
Midway, Utah 84049
(801) 654-1791

There has been a bustling growth in cross-country activity at this 25,000-acre state park in the Heber Valley. Marked loop trails have been laid out over the rolling golf course. There are no marked trails as you move into the rest of the park, but the country is open for touring. Snowmobilers will be found on two unplowed roads that climb up into the high country around the park base.

A rustic mountain chalet with fireplace can be reserved through the park by private parties for a rental fee. It makes an excellent base of operations for large groups, and there is good ski-touring terrain around it.

To reach the park take Interstate-80 east from Salt Lake City. After passing Park City, take the U.S. 40 turnoff to Heber City. As you approach Heber City, watch for signs to the park.

Privately Operated Ski Facilities

> Powder Mountain
> P.O. Box 110
> Eden, Utah 84310
> (801) 745-3771

Miles and miles of high country terrain ideally suited to cross-country skiing surround Powder Mountain. Just be sure if you plan a long trek across it that you are properly equipped and that you have a map and know how to use it. The mountain management believes that more often than necessary ski tourers "suffer" the rapture of the snow, turn up lost, and a search-and-rescue mission needs to be mounted. So if you want to stay on the good side of Powder Mountain, be a thoughtful and prepared cross-country skier.

For a $3 registration fee you receive an area map showing grades and type of terrain. There is no rental equipment, however, and no instruction. You have to make arrangements for those services back in the cities before you leave.

To drive to Powder Mountain from Salt Lake City, take I-15 north to the Ogden 12th Street exit. Turn east toward the mountains through Ogden Canyon, and follow the signs to Powder Mountain.

There is lodging for 28 at the Coalition Lodge, (801) 745-3779, and food and other facilities in the Powder Town Center. Additional lodging can be obtained in Ogden or in Salt Lake City, 55 miles southwest.

> Snow Basin
> 5395 Old Post Road
> Ogden, Utah 84403
> (801) 392-9196
> (801) 621-2234—at Snow Basin

This downhill day area, located 16 miles outside of Ogden, maintains two 4½-mile trails for ski tourers. The terrain crossed by the trails calls for at least intermediate technique. There is no trail charge.

The Ski and Cycle Haus at the mountain and in Ogden has rental skis at $5 a day. The ski school offers instruction to groups for $4 per person.

There is food at the mountain, but lodging must be obtained in Ogden.

Wasatch Mountain Touring Company
779 East 3rd Street South
Salt Lake City, Utah 84102
(801) 359-9361

This mountain shop in downtown Salt Lake City is a ski-tourer's central for the Wasatch. Here you can get equipment and information, arrange for instruction or guided tours, join with other ski tourers to form a touring party, be directed to the training and touring track at Park City golf course, or set off to explore any of hundreds of miles of trails and roads in the Wasatch National Forest. Overnight and multi-day tours also may be arranged.

Lessons are $7.50 per person for a half-day and $12 for a full day. Equipment rents for $5, with a $2 fee for each additional day. From December to March a ski clinic is offered free to beginners each Saturday.

White Pine Ski Touring Center
P.O. Box 417
Park City, Utah 84060
(801) 649-8701

You can get it all together at the Center, which provides rentals, lessons, track skiing, and day and longer tours in the Wasatch and Uinta mountains. To get to Park City and the Center, go east from Salt Lake City on Interstate-80 for about 20 miles to the Park City cutoff. It's another 6 miles to Park City. The Center, which is at the Park City golf course, is in the first building as you enter town. (Their headquarters is the pro shop in summer.) There are one-, three-, and five-kilometer marked and maintained tracks on the rolling golf course grounds.

A half-day group lesson runs $7. An all-day guided tour costs $13. You can combine a half-day lesson and a half-day tour for $12. About one-fifth of the 100 kilometers of marked trails surrounding Park City is maintained. A $1 donation is suggested to support this program. Off-trail skiing is unlimited but should be pursued with due caution because of possible avalanche danger. (White Pine's guides and instructors are certified members of the Intermountain Ski Instructors Association.)

The Center runs day tours into White Pine Canyon and to Lake Flat, Deer Valley, and Thaynes Canyon. Low areas of the Uinta also are covered in day tours. A long day tour requiring intermediate or advanced technique is a 26-mile trek on the top of the high country to Brighton Ski Bowl and back. Two days and $40 for food and lodging will take you on a ski tour to Alta, with one night spent in Brighton. The Center's three-day tour goes to the East Fork of the Bear River in the Uinta. The fee is $50 for food and lodging in heated cabins. You just need to bring your clothing and personal gear in a day pack.

On one weekend each month an overnight touring clinic is conducted. Instruction is given in avalanche safety and rescue techniques, route selection, survival techniques, and snow shelter building. The Center also holds citizen races every other weekend throughout the season.

Alta/Brighton/Snowbird

These three Alpine ski areas are grouped together here because for cross-country skiers they form an interrelated base area through a complex of trails and routes. To contact them individually, write or call:

Alta Ski Lifts
Alta, Utah 84070
(801) 742-3333

Brighton Ski Bowl
Brighton, Utah 84121
(801) 359-3283

Snowbird Ski Resort
Snowbird, Utah 84070
(801) 742-2222

To drive to them, leave Salt Lake City heading south on Wasatch Boulevard, which runs along the base of the range. Watch for the turn to Big Cottonwood Canyon. It will take you to Brighton. Farther along comes Little Cottonwood Canyon. Climbing up into the Wasatch, you first will reach Snowbird and a few miles later, Alta.

Now a word to the wise cross-country skier. There is no developed touring center or organized trail system at any of these three resorts, as there is in Park City. And though rental equipment and group instruction are available, this should not be interpreted as active encouragement of ski tourers. The reasons are quite simple. The terrain is essentially alpine, expert technique often is required, and the heavy snow conditions pose very real avalanche dangers.

You can obtain a map from the Forest or the base-area operators that will show you miles and miles of approximate touring routes running along the back of the high country and shooting down the draws to the canyon bottoms. The routes are approximate because it is imperative that the exact route of each tour be selected for existing snow and avalanche conditions. If you know the country and are an experienced and prepared ski tourer, have fun. If not, it is best to have a guide.

Equipment can be rented for $6 to $7 a day. The ski schools have a few cross-country instructors, but unless you want to pay private lesson rates, you should form your own groups. Brighton charges $6 per person in a class of five or more for a two-hour lesson.

Along the canyon bottoms you will find cross-country opportunities, but there are no marked and maintained trails. The routes on the Forest Service map, linking Big and Little Cottonwood canyons, call for stiff climbing and expert technique. The routes linking Alta and Brighton can be reached by riding lifts. The single ride fee at Brighton is $1. At Alta it is $1.25. Snowbird brings their ski-tour instruction groups to Alta.

Two shops in Alta, Deep Powder House and Snow Pine Lodge, rent equipment. The sole cross-country ski school instructor charges $6 for a two-hour morning lesson in technique and $6 for a two-hour guided tour in the Albion Basin reached by the Albion lift. Snowbird cross-country groups also use the Albion Basin area.

This system of trails and routes linking these separate, developed areas as well as Park City is unique in the West. It brings a European flavor to this rugged alpine area. Treat it with respect and caution and you will have some of your best cross-country experiences. Anything less could well endanger you as well as expose the search-and-rescue teams to difficult and dangerous work.

Brian Head
P.O. Box 38
Cedar City, Utah 84720
(801) 586-4636

This new ski town is tucked in the southwest corner of Utah in spectacular skiing country. We noted it earlier when discussing Cedar Breaks National Monument, which is just miles away.

Brian Head offers the best basing area for trips into Cedar Breaks and can provide up-to-date snow condition information since the Cedar Breaks visitor's center is closed in winter. You can arrange for a guided trip along a generally unplowed road that leads into Cedar Breaks from the north end of the monument. Other places to tour ski besides Cedar Breaks are to the top of Brian Peak, to the Twisted Forest, to Dry Lakes, and through the proposed Ashdown Gorge Wilderness area.

There is excellent cross-country skiing terrain around Brian Head—they use the figure 2,500 square miles—which sits on the edge of the Dixie National Forest. The town is at 9,250 feet, and the high plateau is rolling country. Most of the day tours from Brian Head climb up into even higher country.

8 — New Mexico and Arizona: Forests, Parks, and Private Ski Areas

If New Mexico and Arizona bring to mind only Gila monsters, cactus, dry-as-dust deserts, think again. The Rockies in major bumps and lumps of ranges are spotted throughout the two states but particularly in their northern regions.

These forested elevations, which at their peaks top out above 12,000 feet, force the winter storm systems to climb. They catch the precipitation as snow. It might surprise you, but winter in the generally sunny mountains of Arizona and New Mexico runs from December into April, and that is about as long as you need to have a successful winter season for downhillers and cross-country types. Admittedly, conditions are more variable here than in the northern Rockies. It pays to check before traveling.

Most but not all of the skiable terrain of the two states is Forest Service land. The north rim of the Grand Canyon is U.S. Park Service land—it is open to ski touring when there is snow—and some of the private ski area operators have extensive holdings. Most of these operations, however, abut or move onto Forest Service land for much of their downhill and

A New Mexico winter in the Santa Fe National Forest usually runs from December to April. *Mark Nohl/New Mexico Tourist Division*

cross-country skiing. In just a bit we will note who these private operators are so that you can contact them for information, assistance, ski rental, and lodging. But there is nothing to keep you from directly contacting national forest offices or the ranger districts on these forests. The land is yours and there for the skiing.

We will list here the national forests that generally get good snow cover in the two states. Start with them to find out about snow conditions and to determine which ranger districts to call for more detailed information. All the national forests welcome ski tourers, even in their wilderness areas. But winter or summer you will need a wilderness area permit from the proper ranger station. That's no problem. And that way you will be sure to tell them where you are going and when you are due back.

National Forests and Parks: Arizona

Arizona's good-snow national forests are the Apache, the Coconino, and the Kaibab. One end of this high country starts with the Apache National Forest, which stretches along Arizona's eastern border. From there this dominant Arizona range runs northwestward, linking through the Sitgreaves National Forest to the Coconino and Kaibab, which surround Flagstaff. Snaking down its northeast face is the Little Colorado River. The range itself, north of the San Francisco Peaks, is gouged by the Grand Canyon gorge of the Colorado River.

Here are the addresses and phone numbers of these forests:

Apache-Sitgreaves National Forest
P.O. Box 640
Springerville, Arizona 85938
(602) 333-4301

The Springerville Ranger District includes a tour-skiing area on its territory near Greer. More about that in the listing of private Arizona operators below. You can call the district ranger's office directly at (602) 333-4372. He can report only on his district. The recreation officer at the forest office can give you a snow report for the entire Apache-Sitgreaves, but he might suggest you call a specific ranger district for a more detailed area report.

Coconino National Forest
114 North San Francisco Street
P.O. Box 1268
Flagstaff, Arizona 86001
(602) 774-5261

Kaibab National Forest
800 South 6th Street
Williams, Arizona 86046
(602) 635-2681

The northern section of Kaibab National Forest is split by Grand Canyon National Park. During the winter, the North Rim of the Grand Canyon usually has sufficient snow for ski tourers. A road that is closed in the winter runs south from

Jacob Lake on the Kaibab to the North Rim. Tours can be organized through a guide service in Flagstaff; more on that below. For a report on Grand Canyon North Rim snow conditions call Park Headquarters on the South Rim at (602) 638-2411.

If a ski-tour workout in the bright winter sun of Arizona is something you know you must do, here are the cross-country areas operating on public or private land. Also listed are the guide services you can contact if your interests go beyond part- or full-day runs on marked and maintained rolling trails.

Privately Operated Ski Facilities: Arizona

Arizona Snow Bowl
P.O. Box 158
Flagstaff, Arizona 86002
(602) 774-0562

The Arizona Snow Bowl is tucked in on the west side of the San Francisco Peaks, which run northwest from Flagstaff and are dominated by Humphrey's Peak at an elevation of 12,670. The base lodge and parking are at 9,500 feet. If you should want to mix some downhill with your touring, there is a chairlift, a Pomalift, and some smaller lifts.

Starting out near the lodge and running over gently rolling terrain of open meadow mixed with groves of pine and aspen is a 6.5-kilometer (3.8-mile) loop track. There is no fee for using the track or parking.

There is food service at the lodge but no overnight facilities. Flagstaff, however, is only 14 miles away. To get to the Arizona Snow Bowl, take U.S. 180 northwest out of Flagstaff for 7 miles. A right turn onto a marked Forest Service road and 7 more miles will bring you to the lodge. Just as you leave U.S. 180 there is Forest Service parking and ski-touring terrain available at the base of the mountains.

Skis, poles, and boots rent for $6 on weekdays and $8 on weekends and holidays. After 12:30 the price drops $1. Instruction is available, and guided day tours can be arranged for more rugged country near the top of Mt. Humphrey. You can be reasonably confident of good snow from mid-December to mid-April. The typical daily temperature range runs from about zero to 35 degrees; sunny days are a regular event.

Sacred Mountain Ski Tours
406 South Beaver Street
Flagstaff, Arizona 86001
(602) 774-7809

Based in Lee Dexter's Alpineer ski shop in Flagstaff, Sacred Mountain Ski Tours offers daily instruction tours at $10 for a five-hour run. They have miles of nearby, prepared trails crossing private land; the instructors seek out the good snow. Sacred Mountain also offers longer, catered-type ski-touring trips and ski-mountaineering adventures. Call ahead to make reservations for both daily instruction and the more extended trips. Lee Dexter and the other five instructor/guides on tap through Sacred Mountain all are members of the Professional Ski Instructors Association and are certified through the Rocky Mountain Ski Instructors Association.

The country southeast of Flagstaff on the Coconino is high, rolling plateau with elevations running between 7,000 and 9,000 feet. The ski-touring possibilities here are nearly endless. And if that's where the best snow is, your day-tour instructor might well take you there. When you have become familiar with the area, you and your companions might wish to venture out into the vast, pleasant country on your own.

Sacred Mountain's emphasis is on instruction. There are guided avalanche awareness tours, moonlight tours, and any number of longer tours and mountaineering trips. For $20 a day per person you can take a weekend ski-mountaineering trip into the San Francisco Peaks northwest of Flagstaff. A four- to five-day ski-tour adventure that Sacred Mountain can arrange and lead for groups of up to five people (in top physical condition) is to and along the North Rim of the Grand Canyon. The trek runs south from Jacobs Lake on the Kiabab over a 40-mile closed Forest Service/Park Service road. There are appropriate detours and side trips for the scenery. You emerge on the North Rim, where the Kaibab Trail rises up from the gorge. From there it is a 21-mile walking hike down to the river—where it might be warm enough to grab a swim in a sun-heated pool—and then a strenuous climb up to the South Rim and Bright Angel Lodge.

Skis, waxed and waxless, boots, and poles are available at the Alpineer for $6 a day. Package deals that include motel lodging at special rates can be arranged for ski-tour student groups.

Mormon Lake Ski Touring Center
Mormon Lake, Arizona 86038
(602) 354-2240—Touring Center
(602) 354-2227—Mormon Lodge

About 30 miles south of Flagstaff via state route 487 is Mormon Lake, a 3-mile wide watery or icy expanse in the middle of a 7,200-foot-high mountain basin. Meadow and mountain scenery ring the lake, as do ski-touring trails of ascending levels of difficulty. On the southwest shore of the lake, which is in the Coconino National Forest, is Mormon Lodge. It goes back to the turn of the century. The Mormon Lake Ski Touring Center, which has a much more recent history, is located there. Mark Brown and his wife, Deanna, own and operate the Center.

All 70 miles of the marked and maintained trails start and end back at the lodge. Beginner trails run about the lake. More expert skiers are taken up into the surrounding high, rugged mountain wilderness.

A pair of skis from the Center's supply of 300, as well as poles and boots, costs $8 per day. Midweek, a two-hour lesson runs $4, but on the weekend the price jumps to $6. A special two-day program that includes instruction in winter camping techniques runs $26, with equipment included.

The old lodge has a massive stone fireplace that makes for a great end-of-the-day rest and relaxation area. Accommodations at Mormon Lake range from fireplace-heated rustic cabins to modern motel units.

Greer Ski Trails
Chamber of Commerce
P.O. Box 254
Greer, Arizona 85927

This beginner-to-expert patern of cross-country ski-touring trails is laid out along old logging roads that run through the Apache National Forest about two miles away from the town of Greer. The recreation area was developed and is maintained under a special use permit by the Greer Chamber of Commerce, led by its president, Clark Haslett. He also runs the Circle B Market. Both waxed and waxless skis can be rented for $7 a day at the market. The address is P.O. Box 128, Greer, Arizona 85927. For snow reports call Haslett at the market: (602) 735-7540. Or call directly to the Springerville Ranger District.

Travel time from Flagstaff is four and a half hours. Go east on Interstate-40 to Holbrook, and then turn south on U.S. 180 through St. Johns to Springerville. From there, go east on state 260 for about ten miles to the marked ski area.

Instruction can be had on weekends for $8 for a half-day. Trail maps are available free from the Chamber and the Circle B Market, which also stocks a range of cross-country skiing supplies, including food of course. There are 200 overnight accommodations available in Greer.

So much for Arizona. But it is a certainty that in a few more years there will be many more ski-touring trails marked out on national forests and private lands. There is a booming interest in the sport, there are great expanses of ideal terrain, and the deep snow/warm sun combination of Arizona High Country is hard to beat. New Mexico offers much of the same. Let's start with the national forests and then look at the private operations.

National Forests: New Mexico

The snow-catching mountains of New Mexico are clustered in the middle of the northern half of the state. These ranges are all to the east of the Continental Divide. New Mexico's two

Cross-country skiing in the Santa Fe National Forest, New Mexico. *Mark Nohl/ New Mexico Tourist Division*

major cities, Albuquerque and Santa Fe, both have downhill ski areas on their doorsteps. No winter season goes by now without an increasing number of cross-country skiers turning up in all of the state's downhill ski resorts, seeking some untracked snow away from the base area and crowded runs.

The New Mexico national forests that have the best snow are the Carson and the Santa Fe. The snow on the Cibola generally is marginal although more than sufficiently skiable amounts catch and stick at Mt. Taylor and Sandia Peak. The addresses and phone numbers for these resorts are:

Carson National Forest
P.O. Box 558
Taos, New Mexico 87571
(505) 758-2238

Santa Fe National Forest
P.O. Box 1689
Santa Fe, New Mexico 87501
(505) 988-6327

Cibola National Forest
10308 Candelaria, N.E.
Albuquerque, New Mexico 87112
(505) 766-2185

The recreation ranger at these forest offices will be able to fill you in on snow conditions generally. If you want to know about a particular region of the forest, he probably will direct you to a ranger district. On the Carson the ranger districts with the best snow probably will be the Penasco (505) 587-2255, Taos (505) 758-2911, Tres Piedras (505) 758-3243, and Questa (505) 586-0520.

On the Sandia Ranger District of the Cibola is the Sandia Peak Ski Area, about 15 miles northeast of Albuquerque. Downhillers reach the 10,360-foot summit by the longest tram ride in the world, on the west side of the mountain. The east face is served by chairlifts. Cross-country classes now are offered at Sandia Peak through the athletic department of the University of New Mexico. Call Klaus Weber at the university: (505) 277-5423. Information and ski rentals can be obtained from Albuquerque sport shops: Gardenswartz Sports (505) 265-7787, and Mountain Sports, (505) 265-6949.

Seventy-five miles to the west of Albuquerque on Interstate-40 is the isolated, snowy phenomenon of Mt. Taylor. This 11,300-foot mountain, like Sandia Peak, also is on the Cibola. Information on conditions can be obtained by calling the Grants ranger station, (505) 287-8833. Trails are not marked or maintained, but there are approximately 10 square miles of mostly open land on the western shoulder of the mountain. The old logging roads in the area might be blocked by downed timber. Snowmobilers also visit the area, which averages between 40 and 50 inches of snow annually and has a season that runs from late December to late March. It is about a 25-mile trip north from Grants on N.M. 547 to the Mt. Taylor parking area. If you stop at the ranger district office that is on N.M. 547 in Grants, they will be glad to discuss the area with you and mark your 7.5-minute-series topographic map.

As in Arizona and other states we have looked at, there are almost endless stretches of skiable terrain on the Carson and Santa Fe National Forests of New Mexico. Find some proper parking, take your map and compass, and off you go. But since it's nice to have a base of operations that can provide food, drink, lodging, and supplies, most people like to run their snow treks from an established ski area. Following is a listing of the major private base areas that welcome and support cross-country skiers.

Privately Operated Ski Facilities: New Mexico

Chama Station Lodge
P.O. Box 86
Chama, New Mexico 87520
(505) 756-2315/2476

Chama Station Lodge sits at the base of the mountain road leading to Cumbres Pass. The pass itself, at 10,022 feet, is across the state line in Colorado and on the Rio Grande National Forest. It is closed in the winter. Chama's elevation is 7,860 feet. Between Chama and the pass is what enthusiasts have called "some of the finest cross-country terrain in New Mexico." In a stretch that runs 2 to 10 miles from the lodge there are a number of marked trails and sweeps of open territory. Instruction and guide services can be arranged through the lodge. There also are marked maps available, showing the trails and noting their degree of difficulty. All levels of skiers will find terrain to their liking.

Cross-country ski rental is available at the lodge, and there is a general store for other needs. A motel and two restaurants provide lodging and food.

To travel to Chama Station Lodge by car—there is no bus service—drive approximately 110 miles north of Santa Fe on U.S. 84. Turn onto N.M. 17 to Chama. You might find the area so interesting that you will want to come back in the summer when the Cumbres and Toltec Scenic Railroad, a coal-fired, narrow-gauge railroad built in 1880, operates on the 64-mile line between Chama and Antonito, Colorado, over Cumbres Pass.

Red River Chamber of Commerce
Red River, New Mexico 87558
(505) 754-2967

Spectacular jet trails over the Chama High Country, New Mexico.
Mark Nohl/New Mexico Tourist Division

Red River is at the northeastern tip of the Carson National Forest. To get to this old frontier gold-mining town, drive to Taos from Santa Fe. Go north on U.S. 64 and then take N.M. 3 for 24 miles to Questa. Drive east on N.M. 38 for about 12 miles to Red River, which is reached before the pass that climbs to 9,852 feet.

There are two downhill ski areas, Red River, starting right in the middle of town, and Powder Puff Mountain, about one-half mile west of town. Surrounding the town there are thousands of acres of ideal cross-country skiing terrain. The snow is good and there is little danger of avalanche. North of the town in Midnight Country there are vast stretches of high mountain meadows. By going up river it is possible to ski over and down into Taos Ski Valley.

You can rent skis and get some guidance or guiding from Road Runner Tours, which is operated by Bill Burch. The address and phone number is P.O. Box 254, Red River, New Mexico 87558, (505) 754-2997. Skis, poles, and boots rent for $6.50 a day. A three-hour guided tour toward the pass runs $12.50, including equipment. A gradual six-mile climb is climaxed by a fast run back into town. There is little ski mountaineering in the area.

Another good source of information is John Miller, manager of Powder Puff Mountain. He personally has ski toured most of the area around Red River and would be most willing to mark a 7.5-minute-series topographic map for a group planning a day tour. He also will be glad to give you a general description of the terrain you will be crossing. He can be reached at P.O. Box 786, Red River, New Mexico 87558, (505) 754-2941.

A view of Middle Fork Falls near Red River, New Mexico. *John H. Miller*

Angel Fire Ski Basin
Eagle Nest, New Mexico 87718
(505) 377-2301

If you have your own airplane, you may fly into and land on Angel Fire's 6,700-foot, all-weather strip. Then, pinning on your cross-country skis, you will have 22,600 acres of privately owned land to explore. This rolling, wooded land in the snow-covered Sangre de Cristo Mountains offers the ski tourer terrain that goes from gentle to tough with everything between.

Inside Angel Fire's boundaries there are several restaurants, and lodging is available at the Starfire Lodge. Cross-country ski equipment may be rented from Mickey's Ski Shop,

The snows of Santa Fe National Forest prove that New Mexico is much more than hot, dry deserts. *Mark Nohl/New Mexico Tourist Division*

which operates at both Angel Fire and Eagle Nest; call (505) 377-2501. No organized instruction is available as of this writing, but it is planned, as the number of cross-country skiers is steadily increasing. There is a golf course that is used for practice and exercise sessions and short tours. The University of New Mexico's downhill and cross-country teams train and race here.

For nonairplane owners who drive to Angel Fire, leave Taos on U.S. 64 east. Shortly after the Palo Flechado Pass (9,102-feet), turn south on N.M. 38. Angel Fire is a few miles from the turnoff from U.S. 64.

Sipapu Ski Area
P.O. Box 29
Vadito, New Mexico 87579
(505) 587-2240

This small ski area is tucked away in the middle of the Carson National Forest. Surrounding it is an array of forest-service roads and trails that area owners Loyd and Olive Bolander will be glad to discuss with you as you study your 7.5-minute-series topographic map. Most of the terrain is reasonably mountainous and will require skills at the intermediate level and above. Sipapu will rent you skis, poles, and boots for $6 a day.

If you head south from Sipapu toward the Pecos Wilderness Area, you are traveling into expert and ski-mountaineering country. Plan ahead; plan carefully.

Taos Ski Valley
Taos, New Mexico 87571
(505) 776-2266

Taos itself is an ancient adobe town founded in 1617. Since the turn of the century it has housed a renowned art colony. Nearby is the famous Taos Pueblo. From the town, the Ski Valley is 4 miles north on U.S. 64 and 15 miles northeast on N.M. 150. For most cross-country skiers there is little point in trekking there. The steepness keeps the focus on downhill.

But there is plenty of good ski touring within easy reach of Taos. West and north of Taos there is rolling terrain to be reached by going out U.S. 64 and N.M. 3. Traveling as far as Tres Piedras at the intersection of U.S. 64 and 285 puts you on the edge of the Carson National Forest. To the west and north of Tres Piedras on the Carson there is a simply huge stretch of high mountain country that rolls on and on and on.

For more information on all these areas and rental lessons, and certified guides, call Taos Mountain Outfitters at (505) 758-9292. Their address is P.O. Box 1862, Taos, New Mexico 87571. Another outfit is J.B. Cottam's Ski Shop in Taos, (505) 758-8242, and out in the Ski Valley at (505) 776-8256. The Chamber of Commerce in Taos now is handling bookings for lodgings in town. Their number is (505) 758-3873. To make reservations out in the Ski Valley call (505) 776-2266.

Appendix

Standard Ski Trail Classifications

The following shape and color symbols will be used on most ski-touring trail maps and on the trail head signs. Trail ratings are based on terrain.

Green   ●   EASIEST—No slopes are beyond 10 percent. Downhill sections are gentle and wide.

Blue   ■   MORE DIFFICULT—Slopes may be as steep as 25 percent, with some sharp turns. Up to one-third of the trail will be uphill. ("Intermediate" rather than "More Difficult" is the description used on some maps.)

Black   ◆   MOST DIFFICULT—Slopes might be as steep as 40 percent, with narrow turns. No more than one-half of the trail will be uphill.

Ski-Touring Trail Map Legend Symbols

The symbols used on ski-touring trail maps vary, depending upon the organization that has prepared it. The meaning of most symbols is obvious. Here are some of the more popular symbols.

 Ski Trail

 Ski Trail

 Snowmobile Trail

 Snowmobile Trail

 Direction Recommended

 Direction Recommended

 Parking

 Parking

 Uphill

 Steep Uphill

 Trail Number

 Avalanche Path

 Public Use Tent

 Public Use Cabin

Winter Back-Country Ethics

The deep back country of the winter Rockies in Colorado, Utah, New Mexico, and Arizona might go years without the tracks of a cross-country skier slicing through the heavy snows. But where roads lead to good touring terrain and trails are marked out, each year has seen heavier and heavier use. One safe assumption is that all ski tourers and other winter sports enthusiasts wish to enjoy the winter woods and preserve them at the same time. To help all back-country visitors minimize their impact upon the land and its animals, a winter back-country ethics checklist has evolved from the observations of concerned ski tourers and the Forest Service. The common goal of all these guides to proper conduct in the winter back country is summed up in the oft-repeated phrase: "PLEASE TAKE ONLY PHOTOGRAPHS; LEAVE NOTHING BUT YOUR SKI TRACKS."

Seek to camp without leaving a trace. The portable stove and foam pad have replaced wood fires and tree-bough beds. If a wood fire is absolutely necessary, use dead down-wood; don't break dead branches off of the trees. After breaking camp, scatter the ashes. If birds or other wildlife will eat some food scraps, fine. But gather up what remains before you leave. Look over the campsite as you get ready to leave to be sure that the next skiers passing that way will never know you stopped.

Respect private property. Always seek permission before crossing private land. If the ownership of the land is unknown to you and "No Trespassing" signs are absent, do not assume access; assume it is private, and seek out the owner or information. Circumnavigate as necessary; use the "Golden Rule" to decide the countless situations you might encounter. The only exception, which is raised regularly in discussions of winter back-country ethics, is a true emergency. The resolution of such a situation is good judgment.

Pack out everything. Leaving trash on the winter snow is not only an insult to the environment; it also mars your very reasons for being in the back country and severely damages the pleasure of your fellow winter sports enthusiasts. Bring along plastic litter bags that you can seal or wire-tie, and pack out every scrap of trash—your own and that of others. The only mark you want to leave on the snow is your ski tracks.

Show consideration to other winter back-country visitors. Everyone out in the winter woods for sport is out to enjoy himself or herself. To achieve that joy, it is as important to be considerate of others as it is to be considerate of the woods and its animal inhabitants.

Avoid disturbing wild animals. Stay out of elk and deer

A picture of ski-touring happiness is worth a thousand words. *Sven Wiik*

winter areas. If you should spot animals, pass quietly or detour. Elk and deer have a tough enough time surviving through the deep winters. If you panic them and send them thrashing off through the heavy snow, it might lead to their exhaustion and death. Dogs are a real threat to wild animals (as they are to maintained trails), so please leave your best friend at home.

Observe personal hygiene rules. Try to make a point of using toilets at home or at a gas station or trail head before taking off on your ski tour. If you must relieve yourself on the trail, be sure to get well away from the trail or any watercourse. Bury the waste matter in loose snow, and either seal the toilet paper in a plastic bag and pack it out or burn and bury it.

Don't add to the hazards of mountain country in winter. Winter is an unforgiving season, particularly for the foolish and the unprepared. If you ski tour in the mountain country in winter, be prepared to meet all the challenges of cold and altitude. Be sure you have the necessary navigation tools and know how to use them. Be sure you can recognize avalanche danger and know how to tour around it. Be sure you have the emergency equipment you might need if accident or weather suddenly intrudes on your ski-touring pleasures. Remember, if you have to be found and brought out, you not only have endangered yourself but the search-and-rescue team as well.

Be extra careful of the land in spring. When touring in the spring, be sure to stay on snow and rocks. The thin mountain soils are very fragile during spring thaw. If you break it with your ski or foot, you might leave a scar that will never heal.

Educate. In ski touring you have chosen a recreation that not only restores you but does no damage to the environment. Educate others to its pleasures and the winter back-country ethics that give it additional meaning and pleasure.

Remember: Leave nothing but your ski tracks. The next snow fall will quietly erase even them. Skiers crossing the same land later will find it as unmarked and beautiful as you did when you passed that way.

Ground Signals for Air Rescue

In the unlikely event that you are lost in the deep back country or have an injury situation that makes travel impossible, you should know the ground signals to attract and obtain assistance or rescue from the air. If you are known to be overdue, there well may be Civil Air Patrol or Forest Service aircraft out looking for signs or signals. Private aircraft overflying you and observing your signals also might pass word of your whereabouts and problem.

You can make the signals in a number of ways, but first, of course, find a reasonably open area. If you tramp them down deep and reasonably narrow into the snow, they will be visible from the air, particularly with the help of sun shadow. You also can mark them out with ash from your fire, with dead, fallen limbs placed in letter or symbol outlines, with rocks, and, if necessary, with live boughs. Once you know your signal has been observed, stay in the area.

Few if any cross-country skiers are lost or even missing for very long these days if they avoid panic. In snow country today there are seasoned, professional search-and-rescue teams with outstanding performance records. But rather than count on them to bail you out, strive to assure that all their search-and-rescue sessions are practice, not the real thing.

However, accidents happen. So make a note of these signals and carry it along with your other emergency gear.

Need Medical Supplies

Which Direction Should I Proceed If I Can Travel?

All Is Well.

I Am Unable to Move.

Need Doctor [Use only in emergency]

Need Food and Water

I Am Proceeding in This Direction

Map and Compass Are Needed

Yes

No

I Do Not Understand Your Message

Whistle Signals
Three of anything is generally recognized as a call for help. As you know, the wireless SOS is three dots, three dashes, and three dots repeated over and over. Three jackets or

sleeping bags laid out in the snow would be interpreted as a request for assistance, as would a sequence of three flashes from your flashlight or signal mirror. Putting up three smoke puffs in series might make you think you're in a John Wayne flick, but it will work.

Yell for help only if that is really your last resort and you have reason to think help is near. The human voice does not carry very well, and you soon will get tired and hoarse. That's why you need a plastic whistle. The sound carries and will not be confused with natural noise. Also, it takes little energy to make a big whistle. But, remember, the woods are quiet in the winter because the snow and trees soak up sound. So try to get out in the open and up high. Get away from running water, and if there is a wind, realize that your signal will carry a long way with it but not very far against it.

To avoid signal confusion, here are the commonly agreed upon whistle blasts to be used by both the searchers and the sought after:

Three—"Help" or "Come to me."

Two—"Hold position" or "Return to base."

One—"Answer my call."

Generally, the situation will indicate the exact meaning of the signal and confusion should be at a minimum. For example, a lost individual or party would use three and a searcher, one. If the lost group is sending out one skier at a time to search along a "spoke" for a familiar landmark, the scout could signal with three blasts for the rest to come. The signal to call him back to the group is two whistle blasts. A search party might use the same signal to call back individual searchers.

A "lost and found" sequence might go as follows. A searcher intermittently blows a single whistle call as he follows a search line. The lost individual or party on hearing the single call responds with three whistle blasts. The searcher responds with two whistles. If necessary, there would be a sequence of single and triple calls until the searcher locates the lost people.

Stoves for the Winter Foods

The advantages and disadvantages of different types of small stoves suitable for packing into the wilderness will be argued long and late over campfires by experienced backpackers and ski mountaineers. Your own experience—or that of people you trust—probably is your best guide. And be sure to watch for new developments and designs in trail stoves. A good, long talk at a mountain outfitting shop can bring you up-to-date rapidly. But the main advantages and disadvantages of the various fuels used in these stoves have long been known. Here is one such list.

Advantages	*Disadvantages*
WHITE GAS	
(Never use automotive fuel)	
High heat output	Spilled fuel very
Fuel readily available	flamable
Stove used for	Priming required
priming	Self-pressurization stoves
Spilled fuel evaporates	must be insulated from
quickly	snow or cold
KEROSENE	
High Heat Output	Spilled fuel does not
Fuel easily available	evaporate readily
Stove can be set on snow	Priming required
Spilled fuel will not ignite	
easily	
BUTANE/PROPANE	
Immediate maximum heat	Lower heat output
output	Higher fuel cost
No fuel to spill	Duel must be kept above
No priming required	freezing for effective
	operation

Advantages	*Disadvantages*
ALCOHOL	
Lightweight stove	Low heat output
Spilled fuel evaporates rapidly	High fuel cost
	Limited control of heat
No priming required	
Stable in wind	

Safety and Comfort Equipment

The wise cross-country skier carries a burden—the things he knows are necessary for safety and comfort when ski touring.

Just what this burden consists of—we are not considering regular clothing or a normal food and water supply here—will depend on whether you are off on a lunch hike or a back country overnight. It also will vary based on personal experience and judgment. But there is a certain minimum of safety precautions and comfort items agreed to by a majority of cross-country skiers.

Following is an extensive list of safety and comfort items assembled from many sources. And sometimes, it must be noted, safety becomes comfort and comfort, safety. To distinguish the actual function of an item under particular conditions might be next to impossible. Combining this distilled experience with your own should help you prepare your own safety and comfort equipment list, which you then can intelligently modify for the particular trip you are planning.

SAFETY	COMFORT
Ski tip, pole basket, binding parts	Sun cream and sun block
First-aid kit, containing big and little bandages, sterile gauze, adhesive tape, cotton, Q-tips, first-aid cream, Mercurochrome, etc.	Space blanket
	Tube tent
	Stove and fuel supply
	Foam plastic pad
	Waxes and scrapers, blowtorch, and rags
First-aid handbook	Spare mittens
	Spare socks

SAFETY	COMFORT
Elastic bandage	Aspirin
Triangular bandages	Spare sunglasses
Moleskin	Wire screen for fire grill
Matches in waterproof con-	(or splint)
tainer	Toilet paper
Fire starter (paper, candle,	Cup and spoon
etc.)	Pot
Map and compass	Aluminum snow shovel
Flashlight plus extra batter-	
ies and bulb	
Emergency rations	
Repair kit of wire, tape,	
pocket knife, slot and Phil-	
lips screwdrivers, pliers,	
plastic tape, roll of heavy	
string, screw assortment,	
ring saw or hacksaw	
blade	
Avalanche cord	
Whistle, plastic police type	
Salt tablets and sugar (dex-	
trose tablets or hard	
candy)	

Wind-Chill Factor

As wind speed rises, it whips away your body-generated heat faster and faster. That is wind-chill factor. A 20-mile-per-hour wind drops 20 degrees above to an effective 10 below. When the wind picks up in really cold weather, trouble can come on fast. There are two possible responses to a dangerously cold blow: dress in windproof garments or get out of the wind. The one you choose depends upon the judgment you make about your situation.

It would be a good idea to tuck a copy of this wind-chill factor chart into your first-aid kit. You might not need to know exactly what the effective temperature is when the air temperature is zero and there is a 40-mile-per-hour wind, but the chart might help you draw the fine line between holing up or continuing on when the weather gets bad.

Related Reading

The best bet for building your ski-touring library is to go to the public library and examine what they have on cross-country skiing and mountaineering. Many of the books listed here should be available in your local bookstore or sporting goods shop. If you cannot find them there, try a good second-hand or remainders book store. The nice thing about owning books that match your interests is that you can mark them up and refer to them when planning a trip.

Baldwin, Edward R. *The Cross-Country Skiing Handbook.* New York: Scribner's, 1972.

Bauer, Erwin A. *The Cross-Country Skier's Bible.* New York: Doubleday, 1977.

Blackburn, Dan, and Jorgenson, Maryann. *Zen and the Cross-Country Skier.* Pasadena: Ward Ritchie Press, 1976.

Brady, Michael M. *Nordic Touring and Cross-Country Skiing.* New York: Port City Press, 1971.

_______________ *Ski Cross Country.* New York: Dial Press, 1974.

Brower, David, ed. *Manual of Ski Mountaineering.* New York: Ballantine Books, 1969.

Kelner, Alexis, and Hanscomb, David. *Wasatch Tours.* Salt Lake City:Wasatch Publishing, 1976.

Kjellstrom, Bjorn. *Be Expert with Map & Compass.* New York: Scribner's, 1976.

Kjellstrom, Bjorn, and Rusin, Bill. *Ski Touring for the Beginner.* LaPorte, Indiana: Silva, 1972.

Lederer, William J., and Wilson, Joe Pete. *Complete Cross-Country Skiing and Ski Touring.* New York: Norton, 1970.

Lund, Morton. *The Pleasures of Cross-Country Skiing.* New York: Avon, 1972.

Martinelli, Pete, and Perla, R.I. *Handbook on Avalanches.* Washington: Government Printing Office.

Riley, Michael J. *Don't Get Snowed.* Waukegan, Illinois: Great-lakes Living Press, 1977.

Steck, Allen, and Tejada-Flores, Lito. *Wilderness Skiing.* New York: Sierra Book Club.

Sudduth, Tom and Sanse. *Northern Colorado Ski Tours.* Beaverton, Oregon: The Touchstone Press, 1976.

___________. *Central Colorado Ski Tours.* Boulder, Colorado: Pruett Publishing Company, 1977.

Tokle, Art, and Luray, Martin. *Complete Guide to Cross-Country Skiing and Touring.* New York: Random House, 1974.

Wiik, Sven, and Summer, David. *Regnery Guide to Ski Touring.* Chicago: Regnery, 1974.

Williams, Wendy. *Cross-Country Ski Waxing and Maintenance.* Chicago: Contemporary Books, 1977.

WIND MPH (miles per hour)	Air Temperature (degrees Fahrenheit)																				
	40	35	30	25	20	15	10	5	0	-5	-10	-15	-20	-25	-30	-35	-40	-45	50	-55	-60
	Equivalent Chill Temperature																				
5	35	30	25	20	15	10	5	0	-5	-10	-15	-20	-25	-30	-35	-40	-45	-50	-55	-60	-70
10	30	20	15	10	5	0	-10	-15	-20	-25	-35	-40	-45	-50	-60	-65	-70	-75	-80	-90	-95
15	25	15	10	0	-5	-10	-20	-25	-30	-40	-45	-50	-60	-65	-70	-80	-85	-90	-100	-105	-110
20	20	10	5	0	-10	-15	-25	-30	-35	-45	-50	-60	-65	-75	-80	-85	-95	-100	-110	-115	-120
25	15	10	0	-5	-15	-20	-30	-35	-45	-50	-60	-65	-75	-80	-90	-95	-105	-110	-120	-125	-135
30	10	5	0	-10	-20	-25	-30	-40	-50	-55	-65	-70	-80	-85	-95	-100	-110	-115	-125	-130	-140
35	10	5	-5	-10	-20	-30	-35	-40	-50	-60	-65	-75	-80	-90	-100	-105	-115	-120	-130	-135	-145
40	10	0	-5	-15	-20	-30	-35	-45	-55	-60	-70	-75	-85	-95	-100	-110	-115	-125	-130	-140	-150

WINDS ABOVE 40 MPH HAVE LITTLE ADDITIONAL EFFECT

LITTLE DANGER

INCREASING DANGER (flesh might freeze within one minute)

GREAT DANGER (flesh might freeze within 30 seconds)

Index